Hannibal's March

ALPS AND ELEPHANTS

HANNIBAL'S MARCH

Alps & Elephants

Sir Gavin De Beer

Illustrated by
AUDREY WEBER

WESTHOLME
Yardley

Originally published in 1956 by E. P. Dutton & Co., Inc.

Westholme Publishing, LLC
904 Edgewood Road
Yardley, Pennsylvania 19067

Visit our Web site at www.westholmepublishing.com

First Printing: September 2010
10 9 8 7 6 5 4 3 2 1

ISBN: 978-1-59416-124-7

Printed in United States of America.

CONTENTS

ILLUSTRATIONS

PREFACE

"WHAT IS HANNIBAL?" ASKED THE NURSE AS SHE WATCHED me unpack a book and put it on the bed-table. For years when I have been ill or gone to hospital I have always had a book about Hannibal at my bedside. "He was the greatest general the world has ever seen," I replied; "and he led an army with elephants over the Alps two thousand years ago." "Did he win?" "Not in the end." Back came the ball: "Then why do you want to know about him?" I was on the point of answering: "Because we don't know which way he went and I want to," when it struck me that the nurse would think I was really a mental case. Or would she? How many people today have heard of Hannibal, and of these how many are attracted by the bait that we know just enough about him to want to know more? Detective stories don't all belong to the present, and one of the finest of all problems was set by Polybius and Livy in their descriptions of Hannibal's march. The problem is almost as old as the story, for even in the days of Julius Caesar people were arguing about it.

For years it has been my favourite bone and few things have given me such pleasure as to take it out from time to time and have a jolly good gnaw at it. I have been deeply interested in military history from the time when I became a Grenadier in the First German War. The Alps have occupied my mind ever since I first took to visiting them, whenever that was. Solving puzzles is my profession as a scientist and my hobby as a historian. So when Professor Spenser Wilkinson asked me twenty-five years ago if I had ever thought of tackling the problem of Hannibal's route across the Alps, he started up an interest which has given me the greatest enjoyment ever since and which I hope others will now share.

The identification of places referred to in classical texts has a strange fascination. Among the earliest to devote themselves to it, I suppose, were the people who tried to find the places in Palestine mentioned in the Bible. Edward Robinson and Eli Smith showed how it could be done, over a century ago, by studying place-names. Then Schliemann excavated the mound of Hissarlik and proved that it was the city of Troy. His example was followed all over the Near East, in Greece, and most of the former Roman Empire. Even in a country as well known as we think England to be, there is plenty of scope for this form of hunting, and the identification of Arthurian sites such as Astolat and Badon are cases in point.

The tracing of routes followed by explorers and soldiers is a further development of the same game. Christopher Columbus's first landfall in the New World has been identified by Commander Rupert Gould by a study of Columbus's log interpreted in the light of speeds and directions of prevalent currents and winds. Similarly the settlements of the Norse discoverers of America have been traced by Gathorne Hardy from the Icelandic Sagas.

Of military marches one of the most famous was Xenophon's with the Ten Thousand, and we are indeed fortunate in that he described it himself, so that his route can be traced consistently. If the route which Hannibal and his elephants took across the Alps were definitely known, his exploit would have taken its rightful place in history, but it would not have excited the curiosity nor attracted the attention in the way it has for the last four hundred years, during which much ink has flowed in attempts to prove that Hannibal went by one route or another. For the ancient authors in their extant works gave only just enough information to encourage commentators to think that they had a chance of solving the problem. Unfortunately, the task of these commentators has been made almost hopeless from the start, because the key passages in the printed texts of our principal authorities, Polybius and Livy, have been deliberately altered by the earlier editors to make them fit their own ideas. Of the long list of authors who have dealt with the Hannibal problem, only three, Comte Fortia d'Urban, Professor Spenser Wilkinson, and Mr. Cecil Torr, have penetrated through the garbled printed texts to the original manuscripts and realised the error, but they were unable to profit from this discovery because they took such liberties with Polybius's and Livy's texts in other places that their conclusions are unacceptable.

Three periods can be distinguished in the study of Hannibal's route. In the first which started with the early humanists, the texts were altered to suit their own defective knowledge of Alpine geography. In the second period, investigators led by General Robert Melville went out into the field armed with their garbled classical texts, to see whether they could recognise the ground over which they were travelling in the accounts of Polybius and Livy. Henry Mackenzie has related an anecdote of General Melville near the Splügen pass muttering that he could not get his elephants over that way. But as a rule these investigators succeeded only too well, and wherever they went they found gorges and rivers and rocks which answered requirements exactly.

The third period was really only inaugurated thirty

years ago by Mr. Cecil Torr, who showed that unless a
return was made to the texts of the original manuscripts,
and the emendations of the early editors were discarded,
the task of unravelling Hannibal's route might just as
well not be attempted at all. His stimulating little book,
Hannibal Crosses the Alps, was savagely attacked by a trio
of reviewers whose reviews and letters in the *Alpine
Journal*, the *Geographical Journal*, and the *Journal of Roman
Studies* together almost exceeded the length of Mr. Torr's
book. I came into personal contact with all three of these
eminent gentlemen, but I never imagined that they might
be capable of such false argument, special pleading, sheer
absurdity, and I am bound to add, specious statements,
as some of them displayed in their treatment of Mr.
Torr's book.

I am grateful to Mr. Torr for exposing his critics in
such a way as to provide a perfect object-lesson in the
technique of controversy. One of these critics in his
attempt to undermine the value of Polybius's *Histories*,
on which Mr. Torr greatly relied, said that Polybius did
not come to Rome until fifty years after Hannibal had
crossed the Alps and was not a historical witness, let alone
an eye-witness of the events which he described. That is
approximately true, commented Mr. Torr, but there
could be no point in saying it except to suggest a thing
which is untrue, namely that Polybius had no opportunity of obtaining good information about Hannibal.
As Polybius lived in the household of the Scipios of all
people, and was himself a soldier and a military historian, and was present at the capture of Carthage, the
disingenuousness and effrontery of Mr. Torr's critic stand
well-revealed.

In fact Mr. Torr's critics failed completely to find the

real flaws in his book, because each of them was so
engrossed in his own pet theory. Yet Mr. Torr indulged
in unlucky guess-work over the identity of the river
whose name he had rescued from the garbling of the
editors, and he was not able to reap advantage from his
work. He also took unpardonable liberties with distances
and times given by Polybius, for, like so many others, he
neglected some of the evidence.

I have tried to profit from Mr. Torr's remarkable
acuteness and from his mistakes and those of his aggres-
sors; but it took me a long time before I could make
anything of the problem at all. Presently it occurred to
me that the differences between the seasonal rates of flow
of the rivers in south-eastern France might give an indication which river it was that Livy described Hannibal
as crossing with so much difficulty. Next my attention
was drawn to the fact that the dioceses of the Church of
Rome in France today were originally based on the territories of the Celtic tribes that were absorbed into the
Roman Province of Transalpine Gaul. This is very useful
because it locates the tribes through whose territories
Hannibal is known to have passed. Then I stumbled
across the identification of the river the name of which
was garbled in the printed editions of Polybius and Livy.
Finally I saw the use of recent methods of estimating
what the climate was like in Hannibal's time. They
enable us to determine how high the pass which he
crossed must have been, since it was above the snow-line.

All this has enabled me to trace a route for Hannibal
which I can defend with definite evidence in some places,
inferred evidence in others and high probability in the
remainder. I hope that I have neglected none of the
evidence. If this essay raises anything like the opposition

which Mr. Torr's book encountered, it will show that the subject is at any rate still alive.

To the late Professor Spenser Wilkinson I am indebted for his early and stimulating encouragement, and, although, as it turned out, our views differed, I greatly regret that I was unable to discuss with him the results of my later research before he died.

Professor M. T. Smiley and Dr. R. D. McLellan of University College, London, have been unsparing in their generosity over the delicate problem of interpreting classical texts. They have steered me away from some of the more obvious pitfalls, as also has Mr. G. M. Young. Professor W. M. Edwards has read the typescript and the proofs and has been unstinting in his help.

In the problems of Provençal philology I have enjoyed the guidance of Professor Brian Woledge of University College, London, while Professor Kenneth Jackson of the University of Edinburgh has helped me with Celtic. The late M. Georges de Manteyer gave me the benefit of his vast store of knowledge on the archaeology, history, and place-names of Provence. For the opportunity to become acquainted with certain books on Provence unobtainable in Great Britain, I am deeply grateful to M. René Varin, Cultural Counsellor to the French Embassy in London, M. Fluchère of the Maison Française at Oxford, and Mme. Dénian, Librarian of the Bibliothèque Méjanes at Aix-en-Provence.

The identification of Hannibal's elephants is a question which involves not only zoology but also numismatics; in the former I have enjoyed the help of my colleague Dr. T. C. S. Morrison Scott, while Sir William

Gowers and Dr. H. H. Scullard gave me the benefit of their expert knowledge of Carthaginian and Etruscan coins. Colonel and Mrs. D. A. Bannerman made an endeavour to trace the remains of the elephant of Maillane for which, although unsuccessful, I am no less grateful.

Mr. E. S. G. Robinson, lately Keeper of Coins and Medals at the British Museum, kindly guided me in the portrait-gallery of the Carthaginian leaders depicted on the Hispano-Carthaginian issues, while Mr. G. K. Jenkins of the British Museum provided me with a photograph of the Hannibal coin.

Sir Harold Spencer Jones, Astronomer Royal, Dr. T. C. S. Morrison Scott, and Dr. Angus Armitage of University College, London, were so good as to help me with the date of the setting of the Pleiades in 218 B.C.

To my colleagues Dr. J. D. H. Wiseman and Mr. C. D. Ovey I am indebted for the results of their researches bearing on the state of the climate in Hannibal's time.

M. Louis Lagnace, premier secrétaire-général adjoint de la Société Nationale des Chemins de Fer Français, most obligingly arranged for his splendid organisation to provide me with photographs of selected places on Hannibal's route; and Miss Audrey Weber prepared drawings from them.

On Miss Maria Skramovsky has fallen the task of maintaining order in a maze of papers and correspondence, and making the index.

To all these helpers it is a pleasure to return my most sincere thanks, and to assure them that they will not be held responsible for the errors which my work contains.

Forward, you madman, and hurry across those horrid Alps so that you may become the delight of schoolboys.
JUVENAL, *Satire X, 166–7*

The researches of many antiquarians have already thrown much darkness on the subject, and it is probable, if they continue, that we shall soon know nothing at all.
MARK TWAIN

Hannibal's March

ALPS AND ELEPHANTS

I

INTRODUCTION

THE MARCH OF HANNIBAL'S ARMY, ELEPHANTS AND ALL, from Spain through France and over the Alps into Italy in 218 B.C. was one of the boldest strategic strokes of all time. The struggle was for the mastery of the then known world, on which among other things has depended the decision whether European civilisation was to be based on the commercial culture of semitic Carthage, or on the rugged pattern of indo-european Rome.

At the start of the 3rd century B.C., Carthage was supreme in the western Mediterranean, enjoying the security of sea-power and trading with her stations in Sicily, Sardinia, and Spain as well as with the shores of Africa. Rome was painfully struggling to obtain the mastery of central and southern Italy, where she had absorbed the power and culture of the Etruscans and gradually forged a federation of small states. It must have already become clear that there was not going to be room in the Mediterranean for both Rome and Carthage.

The clash came over Sicily in the First Punic War (264–241 B.C.), at the end of which Carthage lost Sicily, sea-power, and security. Since Rome had discovered how to turn the Carthaginians out of Sicily, there was then nothing to stop her from crossing the narrow straits to Africa and attacking Carthage directly. There was all the more danger of this taking place because, as frequently happens after unsuccessful wars, the

1

Carthaginians' troops mutinied. They were mercenaries, had no patriotism for Carthage, and had not been paid.

Fortunately for Carthage, a strong and honest man appeared in the person of Hamilcar Barca, a commander who had evacuated his forces undefeated from Sicily in the best tradition of Dunkirk. He put down the mutiny in a war which forms the subject of Gustave Flaubert's novel *Salammbô,* named after Hamilcar Barca's daughter, the priestess of the goddess Tanit.

The political situation at that time had a strangely modern flavour. Rome pursued a policy of cold war during which she annexed Sardinia and Corsica, increased the reparations which Carthage was obliged to pay, and declared the Roman sphere of interest in Spain to extend from the North down to the river Ebro. All this was under the threat of declaration of hot war : a glaring example of power politics.

In Carthage, a peace party was in power, commercially minded, ready to go to any lengths to appease Rome, and even to play the quisling. Hamilcar Barca, on the other hand, had popular support and the command of the armed forces. With these he proceeded to develop the Carthaginian hold on Spain, ostensibly to enable Carthage to pay reparations to Rome, but in fact because he thought he saw in Spain a source of manpower and supplies and a base from which to attack Rome. With his son-in-law Hasdrubal and his four sons Hannibal, Hasdrubal, Hanno, and Mago, the 'Lion's brood' as he called them, Hamilcar Barca soon succeeded in turning southern Spain into a sort of empire where New Carthage or Carthagena was founded. In 228 B.C. he fell in battle and was succeeded by Hasdrubal his son-in-law who, in his turn, was murdered seven years later in 221 B.C.

The army thereupon unanimously chose Hannibal to be their general in spite of his youth, "because of the shrewdness and courage which he had shown in their service". This strange man, whose name means "Joy of Baal", was born in 247 B.C. When only nine years old he asked his father if he might accompany him on his campaign in Spain. Hamilcar Barca agreed on one condition, that before the sacrifice which he was then making to the gods, Hannibal should swear eternal enmity to Rome. No man ever kept a promise more faithfully.

South of the Ebro was the city of Saguntum, surrounded by territory which owed allegiance to Carthage. Saguntum on the other hand was allied to Rome. Subversive activities against Carthage were carried on from Saguntum (today they would be called fifth-column activities) and Hannibal determined to put a stop to them and thereby to put an end to the policy of appeasement by making war with Rome inevitable. Accordingly he besieged Saguntum and took it after eight months. The booty he sent to Carthage, which made the home government sufficiently courageous and well-disposed towards him to refuse to hand him over to the indignant embassy sent by Rome, and the Second Punic War began.

It is quite clear that Hannibal carried out a carefully prepared plan which he had inherited from his father. His object was nothing less than the destruction of the power of Rome before Rome destroyed Carthage, and Rome's most vulnerable spot was in Italy itself where the Roman federation of states was still loose and the Celtic tribes of Gauls in the North were in revolt. The

Boii and the Insubres in particular were smarting over
the Romans' punitive expeditions as a result of which
they had captured Milan and established outposts at
Cremona, Piacenza, and Modena. At that time the
Romans did not have a professional standing army, but
citizen soldiers. Hannibal had trained African and
Spanish veterans.

But since Carthage had lost command of the sea to
Rome, how was Hannibal to get to Italy with his troops?
The Romans never imagined for one moment that he
could or would make the journey of 1500 miles overland
from Spain, across the Pyrenees, the south of France,
and the Alps; but that was exactly what Hannibal
had decided to do. A recent parallel is provided by the
confidence with which the Allies in the Second German
War believed that the German attack could not be
delivered through the Ardennes, because they, like the
Alps, were mountains.

In everything that Hannibal did, he had to rely solely
on himself, for the home government at Carthage could
not be relied upon to support him or to prosecute the
war with any energy at all.

Having decided on his strategy and selected his theatre
of operations, Hannibal followed two principles which
have grown no less important since his day: the seizure
of the initiative, and the maintenance of the element of
surprise. 218 B.C. may seem a long time ago, but the
manner in which Hannibal set about his task is identical
with that which a competent commander would follow
today. In Polybius's description of Hannibal's prepara-
tions I only need to insert a few modern military terms
for this to be plainly apparent.

Hannibal's first responsibility was to take measures for

the security of his bases at Carthage and Carthagena. This involved the careful guarding of the sea-passage across the straits of Gibraltar, and the balanced distribution or deployment of his land-forces between Africa and Spain.

Next came the collecting of detailed information about the countries and peoples through which he proposed to pass. Now it would be called "theatre-intelligence". For this purpose he sent for messengers (liaison-officers) from the Gaulish tribes and asked for detailed accounts of the terrain and the fertility of the country at the foot of the Alps, in the midst of the Alps, and in the plain of the river Po. This was essential for any general whose army was to live on the land without any lines of communication whatever with its base. Today, this aspect of Hannibal's planning would come under the heading of logistics.

He also wanted to know the number of the inhabitants of the various populations, their capacity for war, and particularly whether their enmity against the Romans was maintained. This would be called political intelligence. He laid great store by the local resistance-movements of the Gauls on both sides of the Alps and promised them support; for he saw clearly that he would only be able to operate in Italy against the Romans if the Gauls co-operated with him. He therefore planned a campaign of psychological warfare, to raise and maintain the morale of his supporters and to undermine the enemy's will and power to resist.

The operations began in great secrecy in the spring of 218 B.C. when Hannibal concentrated his troops and addressed them. We should now say that he looked after their morale. He told them that the Romans had demanded the surrender of his own person, their General, and he painted in glowing colours the fertility of the lands into which he was going to lead them, and the friendship of the Gauls whom they would liberate. Moved by the emotions of indignation and lust for conquest, his men then leapt to their feet and shouted their readiness to follow Hannibal. He praised them for their valour and fixed the date of D-day, which was about the end of May. In this episode Hannibal's actions were paralleled two thousand years later by another young general of about his age, like him about to cross the Alps, and again like Hannibal, to make his initial reputation thereby: Napoleon Bonaparte.

In addition to the conventional weapons of swords, spears, and sling-stones, Hannibal had elephants, armoured fighting animals which in the Carthaginian army had taken the place of war-chariots, regarded as obsolete. I shall discuss the question whether they were African or Indian in Appendix A. Elephants were hardly a secret weapon, since they had been used a century before by Porus against Alexander the Great. The Romans had already encountered them in Pyrrhus's army at the battle of Heraclea in 280 B.C. With a mixture of respect and derision not different from that which led the British people two thousand years later to speak of flying bombs as "doodle-bugs", the Roman soldiers called the elephants "Lucanian cows". Romans had also fought against elephants in the Carthaginian army in the First Punic War, when the Romans actually captured some. But the Romans had not yet acquired and trained any elephants of their own, nor had they evolved any effective anti-elephant weapons or anti-elephant tactics. Not only did the elephants' appearance, their smell, and the noise of their trumpeting alarm both men and horses opposed to them, but they were highly dangerous when they charged, fighting with their tusks and their trunks and trampling down their opponents. In some armies, but apparently not in the Carthaginian, elephants carried towers containing archers and sling-throwers, so that in addition to armoured fighting animals they could be described as self-propelled batteries of fire-power. Since elephants operate most effectively in the plains, Roman troops in the First Punic War insisted on camping in hilly country, which restricted their commanders' freedom of action. Hannibal's elephants might therefore be expected to give him tactical superiority.

The principles of deception and cover-plans were not neglected, and Hannibal arranged for diversionary raids by small forces (commando-raids) to be made from Africa against the West coast of Italy, and "cutting-out" operations against Sicily.

Not much is known of Hannibal's staff and brother-officers, although there was one called Hasdrubal, another called Gisgo, and a third also called Hannibal, which seems to have been the commonest name in Carthage. There was a surgeon with the army (director of medical services) called Synhalus, and also a field prophet (chaplain-general) of the name of Bogus.

From Carthagena Hannibal marched his army to the Ebro and then to Ampurias, through the Pyrenees and along the shore of the Mediterranean through the South of France, fighting much of the way. As far as the Rhone, there is little doubt about the route which Hannibal's army followed; but from the Rhone over the Alps into Italy, Hannibal's route has been a bone of contention for two thousand years. It is the subject of this study;

and although the events in question took place so many years ago, that is no reason why precision may not be attained in tracing them, if critical use is made of the available sources of information.

II

THE SOURCES OF INFORMATION

UNLIKE XENOPHON OR JULIUS CAESAR, WITH WHOSE campaigns his can be compared, Hannibal left no account of his great march across the Alps. It is known that some contemporary writers wrote descriptions of it, but they are lost.

On the Carthaginian side, two Greeks described the march. One of these, Sosilos, taught Greek to Hannibal and afterwards wrote his life. We know this from Cornelius Nepos.[1]* The other, Silenos, also referred to by Cornelius Nepos, accompanied the Carthaginian army, and his writings were translated by the Roman historian Lucius Coelius Antipater. We know this from Cicero.[2] Coelius's work was frequently quoted by Livy.[3] On the Roman side there was Lucius Cincius Alimentus who was taken prisoner by Hannibal, and learned the figures of the losses suffered by the Carthaginian army in crossing the Alps from none other than Hannibal himself. We know this from Livy.[4]

Not much is therefore to be learned directly from witnesses of the march, and the bulk of extant information is due to the work of subsequent historians. By far the most important of these was Polybius. Born in Arcadia in 202 B.C., Polybius's life overlapped Hannibal's by twenty years, and when he was a hostage in Rome in 168 B.C. he must have had many opportunities of meeting

* See p. 113 for references.

veterans of the Second Punic War, particularly as he
lived in the household of Aemilius Paullus, son of the
Aemilius Paullus who commanded the Roman army and
fell on the battlefield of Cannae. Furthermore, Polybius
was tutor to Aemilius Paullus's son Publius Scipio
Aemilianus, the conqueror of Carthage in 146 B.C., when
Polybius was present himself. As a military historian
Polybius is almost unequalled, not only because of his
balanced perspective, his critical approach, and his con-
stant search for the causes of the events he described, but
also because of his own personal experience; for in 169
B.C. he served as a cavalry General in Greece, and his
interest in the profession of arms is shown by the fact
that it was he who carried the urn containing the ashes
of Philopoemen, the last great soldier of classical Greece,
at his funeral in 183 B.C. Finally it is known from Polybius [5] himself that he made a journey over the Alps in
Hannibal's footsteps some sixty years after the event in
order to satisfy himself about its details. From all points
of view therefore, Polybius's account of Hannibal's
march is entitled to the greatest respect. To acquaint his
countrymen with the Roman way of life he wrote his
History in Greek. It has come down to the present day
in several manuscripts of which the oldest dates from the
11th century.

Timagenes of Alexandria was brought to Rome in
54 B.C. There his skill as a historian and geographer
earned for him the protection of Augustus. Little of his
work has survived except fragments quoted by Ammianus
Marcellinus, [6] including a thumb-nail description of
Hannibal's march, which is important because it gives
the names of the tribes through whose territories Hannibal passed.

The next classical writer who described Hannibal's march was Livy. Born at Padua in 59 B.C., he became a friend of Augustus and devoted himself to a history of Rome. With a fly-paper mind but without much critical faculty, he collected and strung together whatever he could find in the works of his predecessors to illustrate the glorious pageant of the Eternal City.

The writings of Polybius, Coelius, and Timagenes can be recognised in Livy's book not without some errors in translation. The result of Livy's scissors-and-paste technique is that his work is unbalanced and shows many inequalities of proportion and perspective. Small-scale accounts of the whole campaign are intercalated between large-scale descriptions of particular events. Nevertheless, Livy's History is invaluable because of the details which it has preserved. It has come down to us in several manuscripts of which the oldest dates from the 10th century.

A poet occupies the next place in the series of authorities on Hannibal's march. He was Silius Italicus, born in Padua in A.D. 26, only a few days after Livy's death. His importance lies in the fact that in his epic on the Punic War, Silius [7] took many details from Livy's History and serves as a check on doubtful readings in extant manuscripts of Livy.

Scraps of information about Hannibal's march have been found in all sorts of places. The identity of the pass which he crossed was referred to by Marcus Terentius Varro, "the most learned of Romans", who was born in 116 B.C. The passage in question is, however, only known from the later writings of Servius.[8] The pass crossed by Hannibal was also referred to by the Greek geographer Strabo, born in 64 B.C.

It was impossible for any historian of Rome to omit mention of Hannibal, and he figures in the works of Cornelius Nepos (1st century B.C.), Trogus Pompeius (1st century A.D.) quoted by Justin, Appian (2nd century A.D.), and Eutropius (4th century A.D.); but what these authors have to say about Hannibal's march across the Alps is slight.

Geography was not a strong point with the ancients, but important scraps of information concerning rivers, towns, and the territories of Gaulish tribes were given by Strabo and the astronomer Claudius Ptolemy of Alexandria who wrote in the 2nd century A.D.

A certain number of itineraries and lists of towns on specified routes have been preserved which bear on portions of Hannibal's route. The earliest is represented by the Gaditanian Vases dating from the 1st or 2nd centuries A.D. and giving a list of stations on the route from Cadiz to Rome. The Antonine Itinerary, dating from the 2nd or 3rd century A.D., describes routes from Gap to Leon and from Arles to Tarragona. The Jerusalem Itinerary, compiled in A.D. 333, gives the stations on the pilgrimage route from Bordeaux to Jerusalem, passing through Arles.

There are works on astronomy by Ptolemy and other writers, and a manual on farming by Lucius Junius Moderatus Columella, which by their references to the seasons and the stellar constellations, enable conclusions to be drawn on the chronology of Hannibal's march. These can be checked by the Nautical Almanac.

Finally, there is the country itself, with its rivers, valleys, mountains, and passes, as they are today and were two thousand years ago except for some slight changes indicated by geology. The country is, however, a silent witness, a stage on which the actors played. All that it can do is to supply negative evidence in places where the scenery is unsuited to the acts supposed to have been performed upon it.

III

"THE ISLAND"

T HE KEY TO THE ROUTE BY WHICH HANNIBAL APPROACHED
the Alps is given in the name of the river which formed
one side of the place which both Polybius [9] and Livy [10]
called "the Island". This was a triangular area of ground,
densely populated and highly fertile, shaped like the
delta of the Nile. Two of its sides were bounded by rivers
of which one was the Rhone. The third side was not
water as it should have been if the region were a real
island, but a range of hills difficult to cross.

The river which formed the second side of "the Island"
was specifically named by the early historians: Polybius [11]
called it the *Skaras* (or *Skoras*) and Livy [12] the *Arar*.
These are the names which were written in the manuscripts, the oldest of which date from the 10th and 11th
centuries. But when it came to printing them, they
baffled the editors, who did not know what they meant.
Polybius's name *Skaras* defeated them completely, so that
when Perotti published a Latin translation of Polybius's
history, he adopted Livy's name for the river and called
it the *Arar*, which was well known as the name of the
Saone. Carlo Sigonio published an edition of Livy, and
in a footnote he also emended Polybius's name *Skaras*
into *Arar*. Josias Simler thought that *Skaras* was a copy-
ist's error for *Araros*. This meant that these editors
rejected Polybius's name *Skaras* altogether.

Isaac Casaubon published a printed text of Polybius
and boldly substituted *Araros* for *Skaras*, although he had

no manuscript authority to support this emendation, which was based on nothing but his ignorance of the name *Skaras*.

Presently Livy's name *Arar* caused misgivings because it was known to be the name of the Saone, and Jacob Gronovius asserted that "the course of that river is not such as to enclose an island with the Rhone and the Alps".

So the editors and commentators guessed again, and as there is a river, the Isère, which flows where they thought that Polybius's and Livy's river ought to flow, and as its Latin name *Isara* has many letters in common with *Arar*, Philip Cluver substituted *Isara* for Livy's *Arar* in his book on the antiquities of Italy. His only excuse was that in the manuscripts *Arar* is preceded by *ibi*, and in some of them there is an *s* between *ibi* and *Arar*, making *ibi sarar* or *bisarar*. There remained Polybius, whose name *Skaras* had already been altered to *Araros*, so Cluver altered that also to *Isaras*. Joseph Scaliger followed suit, printing "*Isaras*, wrongly called *Arar* by Livy".

Far from showing any diffidence in this wholesale garbling of the texts, the editors gloried in their work. Gronovius, for instance, boasted that "Cluver, that great geographer (*geōgraphikōtatos*), has very rightly restored the reading *Isaras*, and the ingenious Holsten has shown how the error arose from a confusion in capital letters between ϹΚΟΡΑϹ and ΟΙϹΑΡΑϹ".

The result of these changes by the early editors has been that nearly all printed editions and translations of Polybius and Livy available today contain the name *Isaras*, *Isara*, or *Isère*, and many of them give no indication of the fact that it was not what the manuscripts of the

c

works of either Polybius or Livy contain. In other words, most of the printed texts are falsified at this point.

If this assertion should appear extravagant, it may be desirable to substantiate it with examples.

When an editor publishes the work of an ancient author it is his duty to print in the text what the author wrote, and if there is any doubt about a word or a passage, the editor should say in a footnote what the trouble is and explain why he has substituted one word for another. This warns the reader that there is a problem and enables him to judge whether the editor's emendation is acceptable or not.

Let us now look at some editions of *The Histories* of Polybius to see how the editors have treated the reading of the name of the *Skaras*, and what sort of footnotes they have added. The passage in question is in Book iii, Chapter 49, Verse 6.

> Johann Schweighäuser's Edition, Leipzig, 1789, vol. 1, p. 495.
>
> Text: *ho Isaras.*
>
> Footnote: I have accepted the reading *Isaras* from the conjectures of the most learned men.
>
> *Skaras* is the reading in the Codex Vaticanus [11th Century]; Codex Florentinus; Codex Augustinus [14th Century]; Codex Regius A. [? 15th Century].
>
> *Skoras* is the reading in Codex Bavaricus [14th Century].
>
> *Araros* was the emendation proposed by Casaubon.

In this edition the reader can at least see that *Isaras* is an emendation and not an original reading in any of the manuscripts. This is not the case with the two following editions.

> *Loeb Classical Texts.* With an English translation by W. R. Paton, London, 1922, vol. 2, p. 118.

Text. *hē d' Isaras.*
Footnote: none

   Vol. 2, p. 121:
Text: along the bank of the Isère
Footnote: Polybius says simply "the river"

Teubner Texts. Edited by T. Büttner-Wobst, Leipzig, 1922,
    vol. 1, p 271
Text: *hē d' Isaras*
Footnote: none.

It will be seen that in the modern editions of Polybius
there is nothing to warn the reader that *Isaras* is not what
any of the manuscripts say.

We can now turn to the editions of Livy's *From the
Foundation of Rome*, to see how the editors have treated
the reading of the name of the *Arar* in Book xxi, Chapter
31, Verse 4.

  Teubner Texts. Edited by M. Müller, Leipzig, 1905,
    Part II, p. 258.
  Text: *ibi Isara.*
  Footnote: none.

  Loeb Classical Texts. Translated by B. D. Foster, London,
    1929.
  Text: *ibi Isara.*
  Footnote: *ibi Isara* Cluver's emendation.
    ibi Arar is the reading in the Codex Colbertinus (10th
    Century) and in the Codex Mediceus (11th Century)
    corrected from *ibi sarar.*

  Oxford Classical Texts. Edited by W. C. F. Walters and
    R. S. Conway (Vol. III).
  Text: *Ibi*† *Sarar*†.
  Footnote: The readings in the manuscripts are:
    Ibi Sarar in the Codex Mediceus (11th Century).
    bisarar in the Codex Cantabrigiensis (12th Century).
    ibi arar in the Codex Colbertinus (10th Century); in a
    reading inserted by an unknown hand on the original

reading in the Codex Mediceus after erasure; in the
Codex Agenensis (13th Century); in the Codex
Laurentianus (13th Century).

Isara Cluver's emendation, but the argument excludes
these rivers [i.e. Saone or Isère].

The bewildered reader of Livy may well wonder what
to believe. If he has followed the Teubner Texts, he will
have had to accept the reading *Isara* without any warn-
ing that it is at least doubtful. The Loeb Text also favours
Isara although it is admitted to be an emendation. The
Oxford Texts show that the editors were worried about
the reading but that they inclined towards the form *Sarar*
although many manuscripts, including the oldest, have
Arar.

In forcing the name *Isaras* and *Isara* on Polybius's and
Livy's river, Cluver doubtless thought that he was making a valuable emendation, because Livy specified that
his *Arar* rose in the Alps and flowed near the territory of
the Allobroges, neither of which is true of the Saone.
The first of these statements is true of the Isère but the
second is not, because the Allobroges lived not near but
on the Isère.

There is a second reason why it is unlikely that Polybius made a mistake about the name *Skaras*, and this is
because we know from Julius Caesar that even in his day
the Gauls used the Greek alphabet. In the neighbourhood
of the great Greek trading settlement of Marseilles this
use must have been all the more prevalent. What this
means is that if Polybius on his journey in Hannibal's
footsteps ever saw the name of the *Skaras* written by the
Gauls, he would not have had to transcribe it, since it
would have been written in the alphabet of his own
tongue.

The change from Livy's *Arar* into *Isara* was particularly stupid. It is known that *Arar* must have been the reading shortly after Livy's death, because Silius Italicus[7] in his poem on the history of the Punic War copied Livy very closely and called the river the Arar. There can be no doubt about this because the accuracy of the reading is proved by the metre of the poem. Latin verse has its uses.

In spite of these easily demonstrable facts, Douglas Freshfield, one of the more recent commentators, stated that "the emendation *Isaras* has generally been adopted in the best modern editions". It is a poor judgment of the use of the expression "best" as applied to editions of classical texts that prefers guesses and facile emendations to research directed towards the elucidation of the manuscripts as they were written. With such an example to follow or accompany, it is small wonder that (with three exceptions) all the commentators who have tried to unravel Hannibal's route have followed the garbled printed texts, and their work has been vitiated from the start.

If the early editors were worried by the facts that this tiresome river was called different names by Polybius and Livy, and that *Arar* was known to be the name of the Saone, they might have reflected that it was not uncommon for rivers to bear more than one name, nor for the same name to be borne by more than one river. The *Arar* (Saone) was also called the *Sauconna* (Ammianus Marcellinus) and the *Brigulus* (Pseudo-Plutarch). It is just possible that *Skaras* and *Arar* may be synonymous because *aa* in Celtic means "running water", and *Skara* in Breton is said to mean "to run fast". As for the same name being applied to more than one river, the form *Arar* is also found in the name of the Hérault, the Aare, the Arve and the Aa; while the number of English rivers which bear the name Avon is countless. The early scholars simply could not get out of their heads the conviction that if Livy really wrote *Arar*, he meant the Saone. Even the shrewd Firmin Abauzit failed to free himself from this fallacy when he seriously considered whether "the Island" was not north of the Saone, because Livy said that the Allobroges lived near "the Island", not in it, and he knew that they lived between the Isère and the Rhone.

Instead of making their unsubstantiated guesses, the early editors and their modern successors would have been better advised to find a river which in antiquity did bear the names *Skaras* and *Arar*. If they had looked they might have found that the river known today as the Aygues or Eygues bore the following names in old documents at the dates specified, as shown in the list published by Paul Joanne in his *Dictionnaire géographique de la France*:

Egrum, A.D. 825	*Ycaris*, 1321
Araus	*Aqua Yquarum*, 1393
Icarus	*Egue*, 1393
Equer	*Yguaris*, 1414
Aigarus	*Yquaris*, 1492
Equeris, 1218	*Iquarius*, 16th century
Ecaris, 1272	*Ica*, 16th century

Alfred Holder in his treasury of Old Celtic gives *Icarus* as the old name of the Aygues, and T. Montanari gives *Biquarius*. These forms are obviously equivalent to *Ecaris* and the other medieval variants. Captain Colin gives *Arauris* as an additional name for the Aygues which is presumably equivalent to the medieval *Araus* and Livy's *Arar*.

I first noticed this correspondence in the names when I was reading a study by the late Georges de Manteyer on the roads and tracks of the Rhone valley before the Roman conquest. On his maps he labelled *Iscarus* a river which I immediately recognised as the Aygues.

It is not difficult to recognise Polybius's *Skaras* in the medieval forms *Icarus*, *Aigarus*, *Equeris*, *Ecaris*, etc., and I cannot understand why it has fallen to me to discover and point out the significance of this for the solution of the problem of Hannibal's route. The change in the form of the name is in accordance with the principles of Romance philology which provides many examples in Gaul of the prefixing of an *e* to words beginning with *s* followed by a consonant, as in *scala*: escalier. The *s* then dropped out (as in *stella*: étoile; *schola*: école) at a later date which in the south of France is found to have been about the 13th century.

There can therefore be no doubt that Polybius's *Skaras* is the same river as that which was called *Icarus* in the Middle Ages. The modern form Aygues, as Mr. G. M. Young has remarked to me, suggests an old form *aqua*, and the transition from *Icarus* to the modern Aygues is explained by the form *Aqua Yquarum* found in 1393. The Old Provençal form of *aqua* was aiga, or aigua, and the modern forms are aigo, or aigue. In both medieval as well as modern Provençal the word means "river" as well as "water". It is found in place-names like Aiguebelle, Aiguefonde, Aigueperse, and Aigues-Mortes. The identity of the *Skaras* with the Aygues is therefore proved not only by documentary continuity but also by philology. Of few rivers is such a rich historical record of names known as in the case of the Aygues, with the result that the identification of Polybius's *Skaras* with the

Aygues is not only certain but easily established. So much for Douglas Freshfield and his "best editions" which have emended the *Skaras* into the Isère.

Livy [13] said that the *Arar* rose in the Alps, and the Aygues rises in the Alps of Dauphiné. For most of its length it runs in a south-westerly direction, meeting the Rhone near Orange at an angle of about sixty degrees, as two rivers must if they are to enclose an area shaped like a delta. The third side of the triangle is formed by the range of mountains known as Les Baronnies. The land composing the triangular area is exceedingly fertile and luxuriant, the Allobroges lived near it, and its correspondence with Polybius's and Livy's "Island" is complete. If a paper equilateral triangle, which is the shape of the delta of the Nile, is pushed up and down the map with one side along the Rhone, there is only one place where it fits with a straight river along its second side and a row of mountains marking its third side, and this is between the Rhone and the Aygues.

There would have been no inconsistency in a Greek writer calling such a piece of land an island, for as Professor W. M. Edwards has reminded me, the word which Polybius used, *nēsos*, also meant "land flooded by the Nile", and the fact that Polybius expressly compared the region in question with the Nile delta makes it very probable that this was the sense in which he used the word. The region must have been low-lying and subject to floods which no doubt played an important part in its fertility. This is precisely the case with the land on the East of the Rhone where the Aygues runs into it.

Polybius expressly said that this piece of land "was called the Island". This must mean that in Polybius's day the place had a Gaulish name of which *nēsos* was the

Greek equivalent. The Gaulish name must have been something like *inis*, for the other Celtic languages have an almost identical word which means "island", "place surrounded by water", or "place protected by water", and the water can be fresh water. Examples are: Erse, *innis*; Gaelic, *inis*; Welsh, *ynis*; Cornish, *enys*; Breton, *enez*; Manx, *insh*.

This word has left its mark in place-names in many countries occupied by Celtic populations. Examples in Ireland are: Ennis, Enniscorthy, Enniskillen, and many more, all characterised by their low-lying situation and proximity to water without being true islands like Inisboffin off Galway or Enez Vaz (Ile de Batz) off Brittany.

It must be supposed that when south-eastern Gaul became the Roman Province in 121 B.C., the Latin language was superimposed on Gaulish, and *"inis"* became known as *insula* by which name Livy [14] (like Polybius) expressly said that this piece of land was called. Quite close to it, to the south of the Aygues, is the town of Isle-sur-Sorgues, which may well be a vestige of the name *insula* originally applied to the region as Professor Spenser Wilkinson suggested. Other examples of the word Isle or Ile applied to places that are not strictly islands are found in Ile-Bouchard in Touraine, Isle-Adam near Pontoise, Isle-Jourdain in Gascony and another town of the same name near Poitiers, some seventy villages scattered throughout France, and the city of Lille in Flanders.

Even the Anglo-Saxon word *ea* and the Old English word *iez* "island" also meant "watered place" or "meadow", and are found in the place-names Eye in Suffolk, and Thorney in the Isle of Ely.

There is therefore nothing extraordinary in the application of the word "Island" by Polybius and Livy to the land between the Rhone and the Aygues.

The piece of land enclosed between the Rhone and the Isère and the nearest mountains (the range of the Mont du Chat) is not triangular at all; its land is not particularly fertile, and its vegetation is by no means luxuriant. Finally, it was actually the home of the Allobroges. On all these counts, topographical and toponymic, Polybius's *Skaras* and Livy's *Arar* cannot have been the Isère, or any of the Rhone's tributaries except the Aygues.

IV

THE CROSSING OF THE RHONE

Now that "the island" has been definitely identified and the river which formed its southern boundary recognised as the Aygues, it is possible to trace the story back in Polybius's and Livy's accounts, and to see where Hannibal crossed the Rhone. They both say that it was after four days' march from the place where he crossed the Rhone that Hannibal reached "the Island". The speed of march of his army is given by Polybius [15] as 80 stadia a day, and in order to interpret this statement in modern units of distance it is necessary to consider Polybius's measurements in general.

At the outset of his account of Hannibal's march, Polybius [16] gave an overall estimate of the distances which he covered in round figures. The unit of measurement that he used was the Greek stadion, and after giving the distance between Ampurias and the Rhone as 1600 stadia the text [17] continues: "these distances have been carefully measured by the Romans in units of 8 stadia".

This sentence has led to the assumption that Polybius's stadion was one eighth of a Roman mile, or 185 metres. But the Roman road from the Pyrenees to the Rhone was not built until after Polybius's death, which suggests that the sentence quoted above is a later interpolation into Polybius's text. This view is made all the more probable by the fact that Strabo [18] writing in the 1st century B.C. expressly stated that Polybius counted $8\frac{1}{3}$ stadia to the Roman mile, which gives Polybius's stadion a length of 177 metres 50. This positive information can hardly be rejected, and although it only makes a difference of 5 per cent, it must be accepted as the basis for interpreting Polybius's measurements. It appears that the Greek stadion was rationalised to a length of one-eighth of a Roman mile by Artemidorus, fifty years after the Roman conquest of Greece. Polybius's statement that Hannibal's army marched 80 stadia a day therefore works out roughly at 14 kilometres.

Measuring southwards from the Aygues near Orange, it is 62 kilometres to Arles which lies just above the point where the Rhone divides into its tributaries, and this distance is a close enough interpretation of 320 stadia or 56 kilometres.

Polybius [19] relates that Hannibal crossed the Rhone "where it is a single stream", *kata tēn haplēn rhysin*, "at a distance of four days' march from the sea". He had come from Spain along the coast and must have left the sea near Aigues-Mortes where the western mouth of the Rhone runs into it. The distance from the sea below Aigues-Mortes to Fourques opposite Arles is about 60 kilometres. For the length of Hannibal's route from Ampurias to the point where he crossed the Rhone, Polybius [16] gave a distance of 1600 stadia or 284 kilometres. From Ampurias to Fourques by the shortest route the distance is 289 kilometres. There is therefore no doubt that the crossing of the Rhone was made from Fourques to Arles.

This was the place where the Rhone was crossed by the route from Cadiz to Rome given on the Gaditanian Vases, by the Itinerary from Bordeaux to Jerusalem, and also by the Antonine Itinerary. It was only in Strabo's description and the later Roman Itineraries depicted in the Peutinger Table and the Anonymous of Ravenna that the Rhone crossing was made 17 kilometres farther north, between Beaucaire and Tarascon.

Between Fourques and Arles the Rhone is at its widest, about 800 metres and correspondingly shallow and slow. Nowhere else along its course can the details of Polybius's [21] description of the crossing be made to apply. From the boatmen on the spot he obtained all the available large boats and coracles; and they were very numerous because they were very much used for the trade between the river and the sea.

With these boats and rafts which he had made, Hannibal had enough craft to carry his 38,000 foot soldiers and 8000 horsemen across the river. But hostile Gauls appeared on the opposite bank, so Hannibal detached a force under Hanno to go upstream some 35 kilometres where there was an island in the river, cross over with its help, and march down the eastern bank to fall on the Gauls in the rear. Meanwhile, the horses were embarked on the large boats, or made to swim, the reins of three or four being held by one man in a boat; the men were embarked on the coracles, and the army crossed, the large boats keeping station on the upstream side to protect the coracles from the strength of the current.

Hannibal's thirty-seven elephants gave him a lot of trouble.[22] He built piers about 60 metres long jutting out into the river, and to the end of them he fastened long rafts, covered with earth so as to give the elephants the impression that they were still on dry land. Two cow elephants were led unsuspectingly on to the rafts and were quietly followed by the bulls. When they were on the rafts these were made loose and towed away into mid-stream. The elephants were naturally alarmed and some of them stampeded and spilled their rafts into the river, but thanks to the length of their trunks which projected above the surface of the water, they were within their depth and waded safely across without the loss of a single one. In modern military language, it would be said that Hannibal's armoured fighting animals were "water-proofed for a ten-foot wade". This could only have been done where the river was at its widest and shallowest.

Meanwhile Publius Cornelius Scipio had sailed from Italy with an army for Spain and had put in near the eastern mouth of the Rhone where he learned to his astonishment that Hannibal was about to cross the river. Scipio sent out some cavalry which met Hannibal's after it had crossed, and drove it back far enough for the men to be able to see Hannibal's camp. Scipio's men then promptly returned to him with their information, and Scipio immediately marched up the eastern arm of the Rhone with his army to attack Hannibal. But when he reached the place where Hannibal had crossed, he found that he had left it three days before, which was the day after the cavalry skirmish. As Scipio in his eagerness to get at Hannibal must also have started on the day after the skirmish, he took three days to reach the point of Hannibal's crossing. The distance is a little less than that from Aigues-Mortes to Fourques which Hannibal covered in four days. Even so, Scipio's army covered nearly 20 kilometres a day in addition to building an entrenched camp every night which Roman armies invariably did. This confirms the conclusion that the point of Hannibal's passage of the Rhone cannot have been farther north than Arles, or Scipio's army could not have reached it in three days.

V

FROM THE CROSSING OF THE RHONE TO "THE ISLAND"

AFTER THE CROSSING OF THE RHONE, HANNIBAL RECEIVED a deputation of Gaulish chiefs led by Magil, a King of the Boii, who had come over the Alps from Italy to welcome the help of the Carthaginians against the Romans. This would now be called a Military Mission. Hannibal let the chiefs address his troops, and he gave them a harangue himself to raise their morale, for they were nervous at the unusual prospect of crossing the Alps. He reminded them that the ancestors of these chiefs had crossed these same Alps with their wives and families. This was of course true, because all the Gauls in Northern Italy had got there only by crossing the Alps. Livy [23] has related how three centuries before Hannibal's time, Bellovesus had led his tribe of Gauls over "the Durian Pass", also called "the Taurine Pass", on their way to Lombardy where they founded Milan. On Bellovesus's tracks, Elitovius led the Cenomani over the Alps to establish themselves near Brescia and Verona. The Boii and the Lingones were said to have crossed the Grand St. Bernard Pass. After them came the Senones, and only twenty years before Hannibal's march, the Boiian chiefs Atis and Galatas had called in more Gauls. In 225 B.C. Concolitanus and Aneroestus had crossed from the Rhone valley over the Alps into Italy, as Polybius [24] related. Three years later yet another lot of Gauls was called in.

While it was certainly an unfamiliar experience for the

Africans and Spaniards who composed Hannibal's army to cross the Alps, it was an operation that had been repeated many times in recent years by the Gauls, and the passes must have been fairly well known. With their great general to lead them, their own fortitude, and the friendly Gauls to guide them through the mountains, Hannibal's troops had nothing to fear.

After this interlude, the army set out on its march [25] up the valley of the Rhone "away from the sea, towards the centre of Europe". Hannibal's reason for this march was that he did not wish to engage the Romans in a pitched battle until he could do so on Italian soil when the moral effect of victory would be all the greater. This detail in itself shows how carefully Hannibal had planned the strategy of his campaign.

Hannibal's route lay from Arles by Maillane to the river Durance. Late in the eighteenth century the bones of an elephant were found buried at Maillane, but as a description of this event here would interrupt the story of Hannibal's progress, it is deferred to Appendix A.

The Durance in its lower reaches near its entry into the Rhone is not likely to have given Hannibal much trouble. This is because in prehistoric and early historic times, as Desjardins showed, the Durance did not flow only into the Rhone by a single mouth near Avignon, but by three other outlets. The first of these was a breakaway to the south near Mallemort which flowed southwards to Salon and divided; one branch flowed into the Etang de Berre and so directly into the sea. The other branch ran west by the side of the boulder-strewn flood-plain of La Crau to the marshes and pools near Arles and so into the Rhone below the point of Hannibal's crossing. The course of this branch is shown today by the canal of Barbegal which was canalised by the Romans. Strabo who wrote in the 1st century B.C. described [26] the plain of La Crau and said that in the middle of it there was a stretch of water.

The Greek traveller Posidonios, who passed through Gaul about 100 B.C. and whose writings were quoted by Strabo, recognised the pebbles and boulders of La Crau as water-worn. This is the correct geological explanation of this plain, even if it is less poetical than that of Aeschylus,[27] who made Zeus rain down pebbles from the sky in that place to provide missiles for Hercules in his fight against the Ligurians who lived there.

The second breakaway left the Durance at Orgon and flowed by St. Rémy also into the marshes of Arles. It bears the name of Vieille Durance and was also canalised by the Romans.

The third breakaway was the most important of all. It left the Durance between Chateaurenard and Rognonas and spilled into the plain of Maillane, likewise to flow into the marshes of Arles. Its course was represented by the river Duransole which finally dried up in A.D. 1636. In the course of the last two thousand years these branches of the Durance have become silted up, while the present channel widened.

Hannibal would only have had to cross the branch of the Durance that flowed into the Rhone near Avignon. This could not have carried much water in his day and is not likely to have given him any trouble, nor to have been worthy of special mention by the early historians who made no reference to the many other tributaries of the Rhone (such as the Sorgues or the Roubion) which Hannibal must have crossed.

After crossing the Durance, Hannibal next crossed the

D

Aygues (the *Skaras* or *Arar*) and reached "the Island"
where he found a civil war being waged between two
brothers, with the elder of whom, Brancus, Hannibal
sided to drive out the other.[28]

Polybius did not specify Brancus's nationality, but
Livy [29] stated that the inhabitants of "the Island" were
Allobroges, in which he was surely mistaken and con-
tradicted himself, because he had just said [30] that the
Allobroges lived near "the Island", not in it. This is confirmed [31] by the fact that when Hannibal left "the
Island", Brancus give him an escort to protect him
against the Allobroges. From other sources it is known
that the Allobroges lived north of the Isère, and it must
be concluded that Livy was confused in his views on the
nationality of the inhabitants of "the Island".

After settling the civil war Hannibal refitted and re-
equipped his army with Brancus's help. His troops had
already marched 5800 stadia (or 1220 kilometres) from
Carthagena in four months. They were now issued with
new weapons, new clothes, new shoes, and rations for
many days. They were then ready for their attempt to
cross the Alps.

VI

FROM "THE ISLAND" TO
"THE ASCENT TOWARDS THE ALPS"

F ROM HANNIBAL'S CROSSING OF THE RHONE TO HIS ARRIVAL
in "the Island" the descriptions given by Polybius and
Livy agree in all essentials and many details. But from
"the Island" to the place which Polybius [32] called the
"ascent on the way to the Alps", *pros tas Alpeis anabolē*,
the texts of the two historians differ in their treatment of
the subject. Polybius gave a laconic general description
of the route without details or place-names but with
overall distances. Livy gave details and place-names but
without distances or any general description, which,
with his scissors-and-paste method of collecting information, makes his account rather involved and lacking in
perspective. There is no reason to regret these differences,
because each account complements and supplies what
was missing from the other.

From the crossing of the Rhone to the place he
described as "the ascent of the Alps", *anabolē tōn Alpeōn*,
Polybius [33] gave the distance as 1400 stadia (or 248 kilometres); and from the latter point the distance across the
Alps to the plains of Italy as 1200 stadia (or 213 kilometres). An additional detail given by Polybius [34] is that
from "the Island" Hannibal marched 800 stadia (or 142
kilometres) "along the river ", *para ton potamon*, on his
way to the Alps. Polybius had already mentioned the
Rhone and the Aygues but he did not specify the river
by the side of which Hannibal marched.

33

To those who are unacquainted with Provence, Dauphiné, and Savoy, it might seem that from the Rhone
the route to Italy was uphill all the way to the watershed
on the frontier ridge of the Alps, and then down again.
But unless the route lay along the banks of the river Isère
or Durance all the way, this is not so. The Alps form a
wide belt over two hundred kilometres deep between the
Rhone and the frontier ridge, and from the region of "the
Island" it is necessary to cross first a pass out of the Rhone
valley and to descend again into the secondary valleys
and plains in the midst of the Alps before climbing a
second pass to the frontier ridge. From the distances
given by Polybius it is clear that the place described as
"the ascent towards the Alps" must be the first pass,
leading out of the Rhone valley.

If this were all the information there were to go upon,
it would be a matter of guess-work to determine Hannibal's route from Polybius's distances; but fortunately this
is just where Livy's details of place-names, or rather of
tribal names, come in. Livy's [35] account states that when
Hannibal had settled the civil war in "the Island", he did
not take the direct route to the Alps but, instead, turned
to the left into the territory of the Tricastini, passed
through the far edge of the territory of the Vocontii, and
entered the territory of the Tricorii, without difficulty
until he came to the Durance. Silius [7] described the
Tricastini, the Vocontii, and the Durance as marking the
line of Hannibal's march in the same way.

These are precious details and by good fortune they
are known from another source besides Livy. Timagenes
of Alexandria wrote a history of which fragments have
been preserved by Ammianus Marcellinus.[36] His version
describes how Hannibal passed through the country of

the Tricastini and skirted the edge of the territory of the Vocontii on his way to the gorges of the Tricorii. He opened a route which was impracticable before him over the watershed of the Alps. He broke up a rock at a great height by calcining it with intense fire and decomposing it with vinegar, after which he crossed the *Druentia* and its eddies and reached the regions of Etruria.

It will be noticed that Timagenes made Hannibal cross the watershed pass over the Alps before reaching the *Druentia* which, in his account, may have been intended for another river instead of the Durance, or may simply have been put in the wrong place in his description. But the names of the Celtic tribes through whose territories Hannibal passed were the same as in Livy's version, and the problem now is to identify them.

Although some commentators have been worried by this, it really presents little difficulty, thanks to a principle clearly enunciated by Auguste Longnon. He pointed out that when the Romans conquered the Province in 121 B.C. they preserved the organisation of the Celtic tribes as the basis for their *civitates*. He was then able to show from decisions of the early councils of the Church that there was unbroken continuity between the frontiers of the Celtic or Gaulish tribes before the Roman conquest of the Province, the boundaries between the *civitates* of the Roman province which were identical with the formerly independent Celtic tribes, and the limits between the dioceses of the original Christian Church of Gaul. These limits have persisted unchanged for the most part until today, with the result that the map of the ecclesiastical subdivisions of South Eastern France reproduces the territories of the Celtic tribes of pre-Roman Gaul. I have worked out the boundaries of the dioceses from the late Etienne Clouzot's work and drawn them on the map at the end of this book.

The territory of the Tricastini is represented by the *Civitas Tricastinorum* and the diocese of St. Paul-Trois-Châteaux, the name of which is itself suggestive. It lies to the north-west of the Aygues with its western boundary on the Rhone, extending northwards almost as far as Montélimar and eastwards as far as Grignan. Its capital was the town of St. Paul-Trois-Châteaux which is found referred to in documents of the 10th century A.D. as *in comitatu Tramsinense*.

The territory of the Vocontii is represented by the dioceses of Die and of Vaison-la-Romaine, occupying the territories of the *Civitas Deensium* and the *Civitas Vasiensium*. It covers the mountainous region of the Vercors, extending from near Royans in the north to Malaucène in the south, and from Grignan in the west to the Col de la Croix Haute in the east. In the territory of the Vocontii lie the passes the Col de Cabre and the Col de Grimone, which lead from the Rhone valley to the valleys of the Buech and the Durance.

The territory of the Tricorii is represented by the diocese of Gap, and the old *Civitas Vapincensium* which lies astride the middle course of the Durance with its fertile plain. To the west it abuts on the territory of the Vocontii. In the 6th century A.D. the bishop of Gap, as legatee of the Tricorii, sued his colleague of Vaison for the return to his diocese of the valley of St. Jalle which had belonged to the Tricorii.

Another tribe whose territory it is important to delimit was that of the Allobroges. They occupied what is today the diocese of Vienne, north of the Isère, and separated from the Vocontii and the Tricastini by the Segallauni who lived in what is now the diocese of Valence. Finally, the Cavari were a tribe who lived between the Aygues and the Durance, in the present diocese of Avignon. The boundaries between all these dioceses are given by Etienne Clouzot in the "Pouillés de la France" for the south-eastern provinces.

The correspondence between the territories of the Gaulish tribes and the dioceses of today depends on the condition that between Hannibal's time and the Roman conquest of the Province a century later there was no important migration or displacement of the tribes in question. It is notorious that some Celtic tribes were vagabond from time to time, such as the Allobroges, the Teutoni, or the Helvetii. But there is no record of any disturbance of the settled inhabitants of south-eastern Gaul in the 2nd century B.C., and it may be safely concluded that the territories occupied by these tribes remained substantially the same.

Furthermore, the locations of the Gaulish tribes deduced from the boundaries of the dioceses agree generally with the descriptions of the early geographers, although the latter are frequently vague in their statements. For instance, Strabo [37] said that the Vocontii were "above" the Cavari, and the Tricorii "above" the Vocontii. This is perfectly intelligible if "above" is taken to mean that the Cavari inhabited the lowest ground, towards the sea, that the Vocontii came next, on higher ground farther away and therefore to the north-east, while the Tricorii were still farther away and their territory higher. The Tricastini were described by Ptolemy [38] as living east of the Segallauni, north of the Vocontii, and south of the Allobroges, which is somewhat confused but still a recognisable location.

If Hannibal or any modern traveller was in "the Island" and wished to take the direct route to Italy, he would go eastwards, either by Apt and Caraillon and the Valley of the Durance, or up the valley of the Aygues to Serres and the Durance. But if instead of taking the direct route he turned to his left, as Livy expressly said that Hannibal did, he would be obliged to go north-

The defile of Donzère

wards and therefore to pass through the region of St. Paul-Trois-Châteaux, *in Tricastinos*, and then to march through the defile of Donzère where there is barely room for the road between the cliffs of the Baronnies mountains and the Rhone. This situation is well described in Polybius's [11] words as "beside the river itself"; *par auton ton potamon*, the identity of the river being of subsidiary importance to the fact that his men marched with their left feet practically in the water. He would have continued to hug the river past Montélimar to Loriol where the Drome runs into the Rhone from the east. Now hugging the Drome he would have been led to the ridge forming the eastern boundary of the Rhone valley across which there are two passes leading towards the middle course of the Durance: the Col de Cabre and the Col de Grimone. If any reader is worried by the fact that the river is the Rhone as far as Loriol and the Drome thereafter, he may be reminded that these names are geographical, and that what Polybius said was that Hannibal had a river immediately on his left.

The Col de Cabre and the Col de Grimone provide the first experience of sub-alpine conditions to the traveller coming out of the valley of the Rhone, and one of these must be Polybius's [32] "ascent towards the Alps", *anabolē pros tas Alpeis*. The distance from Arles through St. Paul-Trois-Châteaux, Donzère, and Loriol to the Col de Cabre is about 250 kilometres, to the Col de Grimone about 230 kilometres. Polybius's distance from the crossing of the Rhone to the ascent towards the Alps is about 1400 stadia or 248 kilometres. Further, the distance from the Aygues, near Piolens where Hannibal would have rejoined the Rhone, to Chatillon-en-Diois where the route to the Col de Grimone leaves the Drome is about 140 kilometres. These are presumably the 800 stadia (or 142 kilometres) which the army covered in ten days "along the river". Both the Col de Cabre and the Col de Grimone are therefore suitable as regards distance.

I prefer to regard the Col de Grimone rather than the Col de Cabre as the site of the ascent towards the Alps for two reasons. The first is because the route to the Col de Grimone passes through a little gorge, as the narratives of Polybius and Livy require. The second reason is based on a suggestion by the late Georges de Manteyer.

Towards the end of his account, Livy [40] referred to the mention by Lucius Coelius Antipater of the *Cremonis jugum* as the pass which Hannibal crossed. A contemporary of Polybius, Coelius was a historian who earned high praise from Cicero.[41] Furthermore, Cicero [42] said that Coelius obtained information from Silenos, a companion of Hannibal's. Coelius's utterances therefore

The approach to the Col de Grimone

deserve respect. Livy thought that by *Cremonis jugum* Coelius meant the Little St. Bernard Pass, which Livy rejected as it would have led Hannibal down into the valley of Aosta and the territory of the Libici who according to Ptolemy lived at Vercelli and Lomello, whereas [43] "everybody was agreed;" *cum inter omnes constet* that he descended into the territory of the Taurini, whose towns were Turin, Bene, Tortona, and Voghera. The name *Cremonis jugum* was not used by any other authors nor ever applied to the Little St. Bernard. The name was emended from *Cremonis jugum* to *Ceutronis* by Glareanus in the 16th century as a pure guess, simply because the Ceutroni lived near the Little St. Bernard. On the other hand the name of the Col de Grimone is certainly ancient, for it is found in documents of the 13th century such as the Cartulary of Durbon, dating from long before the time in the Renaissance when it became fashionable to invent classical derivations.

Cremonis and Grimone are clearly the same word, and the suspicion arises that Livy, poor geographer as he was, was mistaken in assuming that by *Cremonis jugum* Coelius meant the Little St. Bernard. If this should be so, then Coelius might still be correct in stating that Hannibal crossed the *Cremonis jugum*, Livy might still be correct in denying that Hannibal came down into the valley of Aosta by the Little St. Bernard, and an identification would be found for the name *Cremonis*.

Be that as it may, the placing of "the ascent towards the Alps" at the Col de Grimone is independent of Coelius's contribution and is dictated by the other data. When Hannibal was crossing this pass, he was marching *per extremam oram Vocontiorum agri*, through the far edge of the territory of the Vocontii, as Livy [44] said. When he had crossed the pass he had entered the territory of the Tricorii: *in Tricorios*.

VII

THE MARCH THROUGH THE ALPS.—
I. THE DURANCE

Before giving the narrative of hannibal's march through the Alps there is a problem to solve, and I shall deal with it now because on its solution depends the conclusion to be drawn about the whole line of his march and its direction. When this has been done it will be possible to describe the march in detail.

The descriptions given by Polybius and Livy of Hannibal's march across the Alps agree in many details but they show one important difference. Polybius [45] describes a battle at the ascent towards the Alps, and another when Hannibal approached the final frontier pass, but without any mention of the Durance. Livy [46] leads Hannibal without any fighting to the Durance which he crossed with difficulty, and then describes the battles in the gorges which are obviously the same fights as those described by Polybius.

Most commentators who have swallowed the faked identification of the Isère for the *Skaras* or *Arar* were obliged to lead Hannibal up the valley of the Isère to reach the frontier pass of the Alps. Livy's circumstantial description of Hannibal's difficulties in crossing the Durance is obviously inconvenient for the Isère theory, and attempts have been made to get round it in several ways. It has been suggested that Livy had correctly named the Durance but that he had got it in the wrong place in the sequence of Hannibal's march. The Durance runs into the Rhone above the place where Hannibal crossed the Rhone, and Hannibal must also have crossed the Durance there on his way to "the Island". Livy's description, it was said, might have been meant to apply to this crossing of the Durance at the lowest point of its course, and not in the middle reaches.

Alternatively, it has been suggested, Livy might not have meant the Durance at all. It will be remembered that Timagenes [36] made Hannibal cross the river which he called the *Druentia* after crossing the Alps. In this case the *Druentia* could not have been the Durance but must have been some unknown river in Italy. In placing the Durance in France, between the territories of the Tricorii and the frontier pass over the Alps, it would therefore be necessary to believe that not only Livy but also Silius Italicus had been mistaken, which is unlikely. Furthermore, Livy supplied some additional information about this *Druentia*, including the statement that when it was in flood it was one of the most difficult rivers to cross in the whole of Gaul.

Nevertheless, on either of these two hypotheses, Hannibal would not have made a crossing of the Durance in its middle reaches and there would be no reason on this score to reject the view that Hannibal marched up the Isère to the frontier. On the solution of this problem depends the decision whether Hannibal was making for an "Isère Pass": viz. Little St. Bernard, Mont Cenis, or Col Clapier; or a "Durance Pass": viz. Mont Genèvre, Col de la Traversette, or Col de Larche.

It occurred to me that there are some facts of physical geography relating to the rivers of south-eastern France which show that Livy was most probably referring to the Durance in its middle reaches.

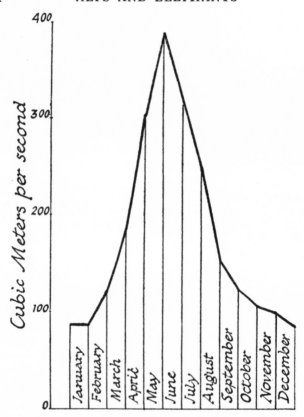

The rate of flow of the Isère at Grenoble

The rivers which flow into the Rhone from the east belong to one or other of two distinct types. There are those which rise from glaciers and snow-fields and have their maximum flow in summer, when the snow and ice are melted. In spite of autumn rains the amount of water carried in those rivers decreases in the autumn and falls

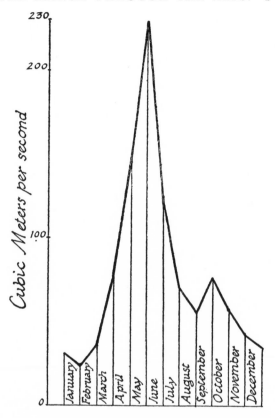

The rate of flow of the Durance in its middle reaches

to a minimum in winter because the precipitations of rain and snow falling on the glaciers and snow-fields are trapped there and held until the following summer. To this type of river belong the Isère and the upper reaches of the Durance above its confluence with the Guil.

The other type of river consists of those which arise

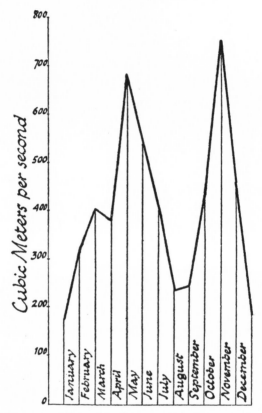

The rate of flow of the Durance in its lower reaches

from springs without glaciers or snow-fields, and they
have their minimum flow in summer, rise in level and in
volume of water carried with the onset of autumn rains,
and are at their highest and wildest in winter. The
Durance receives tributaries of both types, and below its
junction with the Guil and the Ubaye the Durance shows

not only its summer peak flow but also an autumnal rise towards a winter peak.

Livy [47] specifies that the reason why Hannibal had such difficulty in crossing the Durance was because at that time it happened to be swollen with rain: *tum forte imbribus auctus*. The date of the crossing of the Durance can be calculated by Polybius's statement that when Hannibal reached the summit of the frontier pass, it was approaching the time of the setting of the Pleiades. This may be taken as the end of October, as will be shown below. The Durance, then, was in spate about the third week of October. From graphs of the average monthly rate of flow of the river in different places it can be seen that the river is not likely to have been the Isère and most probably was the Durance below the point where the Guil and the Ubaye flow into it, because the upper reaches of the Durance are glacier-fed.

There remains the question whether Livy's description of the crossing could refer to the lower reaches of the Durance where it flows into the Rhone. Hannibal must have crossed the Durance there after crossing the Rhone on his march to "the Island". There are three reasons why this interpretation is improbable. The first is that the date when Hannibal crossed the lower reaches of the Durance was about a month earlier than that of the crossing of the middle reaches of the river. It was on the first day of his four days' march to "the Island". He remained a few days in "the Island" putting an end to the civil war there and re-equipping his army. Then came his ten days' march to the ascent towards the Alps, and as will be seen from Polybius's time-table, six or seven days more passed before he could have arrived at the Durance in its middle reaches. The date of Hannibal's

E

crossing of the lower reaches of the Durance must therefore have been about the end of September, at which
time of year it would be expected that the Durance was
carrying little water, and less liable to be seriously
affected by chance rains than higher up on its course
where its bed is narrower and shallower.

The second reason is that, as already explained, in
Hannibal's day the present channel of the Durance
carried only a fraction of the river's water.

The third reason is that Hannibal is known to have
passed through the territory of the Tricorii; this is represented by the diocese of Gap, which is in the valley of the
Durance in its middle reaches.

I think, therefore, that Livy's description refers to
Hannibal's crossing of the Durance in its middle reaches
below its confluence with the Guil, and that there can be
little room for doubt about Hannibal's route up the
valley of the Durance. But the point is of such importance
that every piece of evidence is valuable. Further light is
thrown on the line of Hannibal's march from independent sources which show that he must have made for
a pass leading out of the basin of the Durance.

In an enumeration of the Alpine passes between
France and Italy, Strabo [48] listed them as follows:

    1. "the pass through the Ligures";
    2. "the pass to the Taurini where Hannibal passed";
    3. "the pass through the Salassi";
    4. "the pass through the territory of the Rhaeti".

No. 1 is the Corniche Road along the coast of the
Riviera; 3 is the Little St. Bernard; 4 has been identified
with the Brenner Pass, but as the Valais was included by
the Romans in the province of Rhaetia, it might have
been the Grand St. Bernard.

These passes are clearly given in their geographical order from south to north, and No. 2, Hannibal's pass, is placed between the Little St. Bernard and the sea, which is logical for a "pass to the Taurini". Since the words "where Hannibal passed" are missing from some manuscripts, it has been suggested that they are later interpolations, which they might be; but they might still be true. This is all the more likely because there is another list of passes drawn up in the 1st century B.C. by Varro which confirms and amplifies Strabo's. Varro's list quoted by Servius [49] is:

1. "along the sea through the Ligures";
2. "which Hannibal crossed";
3. "by which Pompey went to Spain";
4. "by which Hasdrubal came to Italy";
5. "through the Graian Alps".

Of these, 1 is the Corniche route along the Riviera; 5 is the Little St. Bernard Pass; 3 is the Mont Genèvre because Pompey described the pass which he crossed on his way to Spain in 77 B.C. as different from Hannibal's and more convenient to the Romans. We know this from Sallust, [50] and from Appian [51] and Strabo [52] we know that this pass lay near the sources of tributaries of the Po and the Rhone: the Dora and the Durance, which proves that the pass was the Mont Genèvre. No. 4 is presumably meant for the Mont Cenis, for that is the only practicable pass between the Mont Genèvre and the Little St. Bernard, but the addition of the words "by which Hasdrubal came into Italy" introduces a difficulty since both Livy [53] and Appian [54] stated that Hasdrubal crossed the same pass as Hannibal. Perhaps they meant that in crossing the Alps from Gaul into Italy, Hasdrubal was generally following in Hannibal's footsteps, without implying an absolute identity of itinerary. They came from different directions out of Spain, Hannibal to the East and Hasdrubal to the West of the Pyrenees.

However that may be, No. 2 of Varro's list, Hannibal's pass, appears to have been situated between the Mont Genèvre and the Mediterranean. In this region is to be found one of the easiest, lowest and safest passes across the whole range: the Col de Larche. This was probably the pass which Hannibal intended to cross, and it is the obvious route from southern Gaul to the Taurini, into whose territory Livy [55] said that "everyone agreed that he had descended", *cum inter omnes constet*. Actually, as will be seen, Hannibal did not cross the Col de Larche because the pass which he crossed was high and dangerous. This was probably due to the guides' treachery, and he lost his way. But if he descended into the territory of the Taurini, his pass cannot have been far away from the Col de Larche, and it must have been accessible only from the basin of the Durance.

The Graian Alps extend from the Little St. Bernard to the Mont Cenis and owe their name of "Greek Alps" to the legend that Hercules crossed the Little St. Bernard. We know this from Pliny.[56]

The Alps between the Col de Larche and the Mont Genèvre are usually described as the Cottian Alps, so called from King Cottius whose dominions, annexed by Augustus, were in this region. But they were also included under the term Graian Alps, because Ptolemy [57] placed *Eborodounon*, Embrun, and *Brigantion*, Briançon, among the Graian Alps. Therefore when Cornelius Nepos [58] wrote that Hannibal crossed the Alps which were called Graian because the Greek Hercules had crossed them, even assuming that a precise meaning is to be attached to this statement, it does not necessarily imply that Hannibal crossed the Little St. Bernard. It may just as well be held to apply to a pass out of the Durance basin like the Mont Genèvre. In support of this view it is found that Tacitus [59] described a legion's march over the Graian Alps from Turin into Gaul, in which case the route probably lay through the Durance basin.

I conclude therefore that Hannibal's line of march from "the ascent towards the Alps" to the frontier pass must have lain through the Durance basin in its middle reaches, and that the frontier pass which he crossed was a pass out of this basin. The considerations on which this conclusion is based have so much weight that some commentators; who have accepted the Isère as the reading for the *Skaras* and *Arar*, have nevertheless made Hannibal march up the valley of the Isère from the Rhone as far as Grenoble, and have then made him double back again to the south to get to the Durance. This unlikely detour is quite unnecessary now that the *Skaras* or *Arar* is known to be the Aygues, and the Durance could be reached easily by the Col de Grimone.

VIII

THE MARCH THROUGH THE ALPS.—
II. NARRATIVE

FROM THE ASCENT TOWARDS THE ALPS TO THE PLAINS OF Italy the distance was given by Polybius [16] as 1200 stadia (or 213 kilometres), and he not only added that it was accomplished in fifteen days but recorded the details of what happened on each day. For vividness and incisiveness it would be impossible to improve on Polybius's narrative which might apply to a modern operation of war if armoured fighting vehicles were substituted for armoured fighting animals.

It is known from Polybius [60] himself that he went by Hannibal's route over the Alps, some sixty years after the event. Furthermore he lived in the household of the Scipios and he was present at the capture of Carthage. Polybius's [61] version of Hannibal's march through the Alps deserves the utmost respect and I therefore give an extract from it here in free translation, with the addition of details from Livy's account and comments of my own between square brackets to show that they are not from Polybius.

After covering 800 stadia in ten days' march along the river, Hannibal began the ascent towards the Alps, and ran into danger. While his army was in open country the Allobroges hovered around but at a distance, afraid of the horsemen and of the escort [from Brancus]. But when these turned home Hannibal's men began to negotiate difficult ground. The chiefs of the Allobroges then concentrated some troops and occupied favourable positions covering the route by which Hannibal's men must pass. If the Gauls had concealed their intention they would have completely annihilated the Carthaginian army; but they were discovered, and although they caused much loss to Hannibal's men they suffered no less themselves.

Knowing that the Gauls occupied commanding positions, Hannibal encamped near the pass:[62] *pros tais hyperbolais*, and sent out some of his Gaulish guides to reconnoitre the enemy's intentions. They accomplished their mission and returned with the intelligence that while the enemy stood to in their positions all day, they retired at night to a neighbouring town. Hannibal thereupon made his plans and set his army in march again without any attempt at concealment and moved his camp close to the enemy. At nightfall he lighted his camp-fires and left the greater part of his army in camp, but with some lightly armed picked troops he crossed the pass during the night and occupied the positions which the enemy had abandoned when they had retired to the town in accordance with their custom.

[Second day.] At dawn the Gauls appreciated what had happened and at first gave up their intentions. But when they saw the pack-animals and horses threading their way painfully and slowly through the difficult passage, they were tempted to attack the column on its march. As they fell upon the Carthaginians in several places they inflicted many casualties on the men and particularly on the pack animals and horses, not so much because of their own offensive action as because of the dangerous nature of the terrain. The track was not only narrow and rough but bordered by a sheer drop, and many animals fell to the bottom with their loads at each alarm.

It was particularly the wounded horses which caused these panics, for some of them, maddened by their wounds, turned back on to the pack-animals, while others bolting forwards brushed aside everything that they met in the pass and caused enormous confusion.

When Hannibal observed this situation and realised that even the troops who escaped from the present trap would be doomed if the convoy of supplies was lost, he led the men who had occupied the covering positions during the night and raced down to the help of the column engaged in the pass. In the ensuing action many of the enemy were killed because Hannibal fell on them from higher ground; but his own losses were no less great, the confusion having increased with the shouting and the clash of the engagement.

After killing a great many of the Allobroges and putting the remainder to flight, Hannibal drove them to their homes. The mob of pack-animals and horses were then able laboriously and painfully to get to the end of the dangerous pitch, and Hannibal made for the town from which the enemy had attacked him. Finding it practically empty as the inhabitants had all been tempted out by the promise of booty, he captured it [63, 64] together with much that was very useful for his present and future needs, for it included many pack-animals and horses and the drivers taken with them, and corn and slaughter-animals sufficient to feed his army for two or three days. Most important of all, he imposed a healthy respect on the enemy with the result that none dared to attack him light-heartedly on his ascent to the Alps.

Hannibal encamped in the town and stayed there one

whole day [third day] before setting out again on his march.

[Fourth to seventh day.] On the following day Hannibal led his army in comparative safety [Livy [65]: marching in open country, *campestri maxime itinere*] but on the fourth day [after leaving the town] he again ran into danger. The peoples who lived on his line of march had conspired to deceive him and came to him bearing branches and wreaths which are symbols of friendship among the barbarians, similar to the caduceus with the Greeks. Very suspicious of this profession of amity, Hannibal scrutinised their intentions. They said that they knew of the capture of the town and of the ruin which had befallen all who had tried to oppose him, and that that was the reason why they had come. They wished neither to occasion nor to receive any harm and offered to give hostages.

Hannibal remained suspicious and unwilling to trust them, but he reflected that by accepting their offer he might mollify those who had come to him and make them more conciliatory, whereas if he rebutted them he would make them declared enemies. He therefore agreed to their proposal and feigned friendship with them. The barbarians gave hostages and supplied abundant cattle, and placed themselves unrestrictedly in his hands. Hannibal trusted them so far as to use them as guides in that difficult country, and these men led the column for two days, after which the local inhabitants who had concentrated and shadowed the flank of the column attacked it while it was threading its way through a gorge with a precipice on one side and an inaccessible cliff-wall on the other.

In this situation Hannibal's army might have been

annihilated if he had not suspected some such critical development and taken steps to meet it. He had accordingly placed the cavalry and the convoy at the head of the column and stationed the heavily armed infantry in the rear. As these were on their guard the impact of the enemy was reduced and the damage diminished. Nevertheless, many men, horses and pack-animals became casualties. As the enemy occupied high ground and attacked everything that was below them, they rolled down rocks and boulders and caused such confusion and danger that Hannibal was obliged to bivouac on a large bare rock: *leukopetron ochuron*,[66] separated from his horses and pack-animals, to cover them as they filed through the gorge with great difficulty during the night.

[Eighth day.] On the following morning, the enemy having withdrawn, Hannibal rejoined his horses and pack-animals and advanced towards the highest passes of the Alps, [67] *pros tas hyperbolas tas anōtatō tōn Alpeōn*. He was no longer subjected to any general attack by the barbarians but fought small parties of them here and there, in front and in rear. They succeeded in capturing some pack-animals in these skirmishes. Hannibal made the best use of his elephants, for when they led the column the enemy dared not attack, frightened by the unfamiliar appearance of the beasts.

[Ninth to eleventh day.] On the ninth day [from the ascent towards the Alps] [Livy: [68] after losing the way many times in impasses, *per invia pleraque et errores* either because of the treachery of the guides or in attempts to find the right way without them] Hannibal reached the pass where he encamped and remained for two days. He wanted to rest the men who had got through with him and to give time for the remainder to arrive. Many horses that had panicked and bolted and many pack-animals that had thrown their loads rejoined the column.

Snow was already accumulating on the summits, for the time of the year was approaching the setting of the Pleiades.[69] The men were discouraged by the hardships which they had suffered and the prospect of those which were still in store for them. Hannibal assembled the army because he had a unique opportunity to see Italy,[70] *tēs Italias enargeian* [Livy: *longe ac late prospectus*] since the mountains were placed in such a manner as to suggest a row of battlements surrounding Italy. He showed his men the plains of the river Po and reminded them of the friendly feelings of the Gauls who inhabited them. At the same time he pointed out the direction in which Rome lay, and in this way raised their morale.

[Twelfth day.] On the following morning Hannibal struck camp and began the descent, during which he encountered no enemy except single individuals who slipped through the lines bent on sabotage. But the nature of the ground and the snow inflicted as much loss as he had suffered on the ascent. The path was narrow and steep, the snow hid the track, and any man who stepped beside it and slipped fell over the precipice.

Nevertheless the troops braved this ordeal, being accustomed to difficulties. But they came to a place where neither the elephants nor the pack-animals could get by, because the track was too narrow. A landslip had carried away the path for a distance of 400 metres, and a recent slip had made it worse. The men began to get discouraged again and broke ranks. Hannibal first tried to turn this difficult place, but the snow that had fallen made any detour impossible, and he gave up the attempt.

The conditions were peculiar and extraordinary.[72] On

the old snow of the previous winter, fresh snow had recently fallen which was easy to get a foothold in because it was soft and not yet very deep. But when the foot reached the old snow underneath which was very hard, frozen and slippery, there was no foothold. The men slid and glided as on wet mud. The sequel was even worse, for when the men lost their foothold and tried to get up on hands and knees, they slid farther on the steep slopes.

When the pack-animals fell, they were able to stamp through the old snow, but when they had penetrated it they remained stuck with their loads by their weight and the compactness of the old snow.

Hannibal therefore gave up his attempt and bivouacked on the crest after scraping away the snow. He then gave orders to build up the eroded track.

[Thirteenth day.] One day's work was sufficient to make the track passable for the horses and pack-animals. They were passed through at once, and Hannibal established a camp below the snowline. He sent the animals to graze and ordered the Numidian horsemen to relieve one another in working at the repair of the track. [Livy.[73] It was necessary to remove a rock. Trees were felled and the wood piled on to it in a huge pyre which was lighted and burned fiercely with the help of a fortunate breeze. The hot stone was then drenched with vinegar to disintegrate it and attacked with pickaxes.] It was only with great difficulty that he was able to get the elephants through after they had endured three day's cruel suffering from hunger, because the summits of the Alps and the approaches to the passes are devoid of vegetation and bare owing to the snow. Lower down on both sides they are covered with bushes and forests and are habitable.

[Fourteenth and fifteenth days.] Hannibal reassembled his army and reached the plains on the third day after passing the precipices. He had lost many men from enemy action and in crossing rivers during the march, but he had also suffered many casualities among his men, horses and pack-animals, in the ravines and difficult places in the Alps. However, after covering the distance from Carthagena in five months and the passage of the Alps in fifteen days, he boldly entered the plains of the Po and the territory of the Insubres. He had saved 12,000 of his African infantry, 8000 Spaniards, and at most 6000 cavalry, as he himself explained in the inscription which he placed on Cape Lacinium.[74] [He had lost 18,000 foot soldiers and 2000 horsemen.]

IX

THE MARCH THROUGH THE ALPS.—
III. COMMENTARY

It is clear that the first battle was fought over a mountain pass, a *hyperbolē*, through which the track passed on a ledge in a gorge with accessible heights overlooking it. Hannibal went up one side of the pass and down the other where the Gauls' town was situated.

That the place was a mountain pass restricts its location to the range of hills bordering the Rhone valley on the east, north of the Aygues and south of the Isère. Through this range there is a pass leading eastwards: the Col de Grimone, which has a little gorge, the Gorges des Gas. Nowhere but in this region can a suitable pass be found at a distance of 1400 stadia from Arles, and I am therefore almost certain that "the ascent towards the Alps" and the site of the first battle was at the Col de Grimone, as I have already explained.

Some have thought that the town which Hannibal occupied belonged to the Allobroges, but this is impossible because Polybius stated definitely that after the first battle the Allobroges returned to their homes, and if this had been in the town, Hannibal would not have found it deserted. The town must therefore have belonged to a local tribe of Gauls who were trying to oppose Hannibal's passage. Whosesoever it was, it must have been in a very fertile district or Hannibal would not have found three days' food for his army in it. This represented 150,000 rations. The town must therefore have been situated on the eastern foot of the range of the hills that Hannibal had crossed. The country there opens out into the wide valley of the middle reaches of the Durance, extending from Aspres-sur-Buech in the west to Embrun in the east. Near Aspres are many ruins of Gallo-Roman settlements including those of the town of Mons Seleucus, known today as La Bâtie-Montsaléon. I do not claim that this was the town that Hannibal captured, but I do claim that the presence of a town of such importance in this region is evidence that a town able to supply 150,000 rations might also have been situated in this fertile neighbour-hood where olives grow. La Bâtie-Montsaléon is about 35 kilometres from the Col de Grimone through Lus-la-Croix-Haute, St. Julien-en-Beauchène, and Aspres. This neighbourhood was therefore within Hannibal's reach on the second day of his march across the Alps, with the next day available for the rest of the army to catch up with the van.

From the captured town, Hannibal had four good days' marching, and the wide valley of the middle reaches of the Durance would have been very suitable for this. The distance from La Bâtie-Montsaléon to Montdauphin where the open country ceases is about 100 kilometres through Veynes, Gap, and Embrun, and this would occupy Hannibal's fourth to seventh days at a rate of march of 25 kilometres a day.

At Montdauphin the route forks. To the left the track continues along the Durance to the Mont Genèvre; to the right the gorges of the river Guil, known as the Combe du Queyras, lead to a number of passes including the Col de la Traversette. There is no doubt that Hannibal would have had a much easier time if he had followed the Durance to Briançon and the pass of the Mont Genèvre.

But he had a very difficult time indeed, and perhaps as a result of the guides' treachery, the army was engaged in a gorge on the eighth day. This gorge seems to have been deeper than the first, for the whole army was strung along it in file and Hannibal was not able to cover his convoy by operating on its flank as in the first battle. Here, all that Hannibal could do was to clear the road

The entrance to the Valley of Queyras

ahead with his elephants and seize a position on a large rock and wait for the convoy to come through while its rear was protected by the heavy infantry, and all along the route the Gauls rained rocks on them from above as well as attacking in front and rear.

The Combe du Queyras may have been this gorge; indeed there is no other at the appropriate distance in the basin of the Durance leading to a pass such as that which Hannibal crossed. At the far end of it is a large rock, 25 kilometres from Montdauphin, in the middle of

The gorges of the Guil

the valley at Château-Queyras on which the present town is built. This is most likely to have been Polybius's [75] "bare rock : *leukopetron ochuron*", where Hannibal bivouacked. The modern road is at the bottom of the

The "bare rock": Château-Queyras

gorge but the ancient track must have been at a higher level where it is known that it ran in Roman times because of the inscription found at Les Escoyères.

If the walls of the gorge were precipitous as Polybius and Livy describe, there must have been side valleys out of which the enemy debouched when the road ahead had to be cleared by Hannibal's vanguard. Such side valleys are presented by the valley of the Col de Vars which opens from the south near the beginning of the gorge, and that of the Col d'Izoard which opens into the valley of Queyras from the north.

Above Château-Queyras the valley opens out into a pleasant verdant basin.

From Château-Queyras to the Col de la Traversette the distance is 25 kilometres, which would have occupied the ninth day for Hannibal's vanguard while the rest of the army came up on the following two days. The Col de la Traversette is sometimes called the Col de Viso, because Monte Viso, Virgil's [76] *Vesulus pinifer*, is only a mile away to the south.

There are four reasons why the Col de la Traversette must be the strongest competitor for the honour of having been Hannibal's pass. The first is that it is very high, nearly 10,000 feet above sea-level. Only on such a high pass could it be expected that the previous winter's snow would have survived the summer and still lain thickly enough to cause Hannibal's men and animals the great trouble which it did. In that part of the Alps the snow-line today is roughly about 10,000 feet above sea-level, and the question naturally arises whether in Hannibal's time the climate was the same as at present. A final answer to that cannot yet be given but indications can already be gathered from four independent lines of work that it was.

Estimates of the general average temperature of the world have been obtained from studies on the former extension of glaciers, on the height of the tree-line, on the analysis of pollen-grains in peat-bogs, and on deposition of the sediments at the bottom of the Atlantic Ocean. They are detailed in Appendix D.

From all these it can be concluded that the climatic conditions in Hannibal's time were substantially the same as at present, and that the snow-line was no lower. All attempts to route Hannibal over a low pass are vitiated from the start by this conclusion, which rules out the Col de Larche (6562 feet), the Mont Genèvre (6083 feet), the Col Clapier (8173 feet), the Mont Cenis (6893 feet), and the Little St. Bernard (7179 feet). So much for the critic who concluded that "Hannibal was sure to rationally choose, not the highest and most difficult, but the lowest and easiest, most southern Alpine pass". Hannibal's guides were treacherous and his theoretical power of choice can have been but of little avail to him.

The second reason is that the Col de la Traversette is dangerous for an army with pack-animals and elephants. It has a difficult approach through a gorge, and a difficult descent, bad enough to cause Hannibal to suffer the casualties which he did, and for it to become profitable to pierce a tunnel a few dozen feet under its summit in A.D. 1480 to facilitate passage. This dangerous descent rules out all the other passes except the Col Clapier which also has a nasty stretch on the Italian side. It is inconceivable why Douglas Freshfield should have contended for the Col de Larche on the grounds that its access "lies over gentle, habitable slopes, cornfields and pleasant pastures". This is typical of the liberties which have been taken with the interpretation of the texts of Polybius and Livy.

Thirdly the Col de la Traversette is one of the three passes in all the chain of the western Alps from which there is a view of the plains of Italy. It shares this rare

property with the Col de Malaure and the Col Clapier.
The former of these is a knife-edge, close to the Col de la
Traversette, but with nothing to be said in its favour
either as regards its approach or descent. The latter is
only accessible from Modane in the valley of the Arc, a
tributary of the Isère, by which route there is no documentary or scientific evidence that Hannibal went at all.

It has been objected that as the summit of the Col de
la Traversette is a narrow ridge, Hannibal would not
have been able to show the view of Italy from it to many
of his men, whereas he could have done so from the Col
Clapier. This is admittedly a difficulty, but it does not in
any way suffice to outweigh the evidence on which a
"Durance pass" is preferable to an "Isère pass". In any
case it cannot be supposed that Hannibal showed the
view of Italy to his entire army, for the troops would not
all have been available.

There is another point to consider. When describing
the struggle of the Carthaginians against their mercenaries in the Libyan War, about twenty years before Hannibal's march, Polybius [71] laid particular stress on the
fact that as the troops employed by Carthage were
recruited from several different nations and the men
spoke and understood no language but their own, it was
not possible to assemble them and address them as a body
"for how could the general be expected to know all their
languages?" The general could only communicate with
them through their officers, and this must also have been
true to some extent of Hannibal's army, which included
Africans, Spaniards, and some Celtic and Ligurian
natives of Gaul. I suggest therefore that Hannibal
climbed on to a rock (Livy [70] called it "a promontory")
to deliver his address and that as many African officers

and men saw the view as could, perhaps in succession.
A wide pass would not have been necessary for this.

Since passes are in general the lowest practicable places
where it is possible to cross over ranges of mountains, it
is not surprising that from the majority of them there is
no view at all of the plains on either side. A view of the
plains from a pass is so rare that it would be a gratuitous

The Col de la Traversette from the West

piece of special pleading to assume that Polybius and
Livy invented it as an attribute of Hannibal's pass if it
did not exist. Polybius,[5] it will be remembered, crossed
Hannibal's pass himself.

The view from the Col de la Traversette has not been
enjoyed by many persons in recent years, let alone photo-
graphed owing to the ease with which triggers were pulled
at anybody venturing on the frontier with cameras at
unauthorised crossing places. For descriptions of the
view it is therefore necessary to go back to earlier

travellers. James David Forbes crossed the pass in 1839 and wrote: "The ascent was over steep grass slopes . . . and from the summit the view was superb, stretching away to the hills above Genoa." John Ball confirmed this: "To those who approach from the side of France, the view suddenly unfolded at the summit, extending, in clear weather, across the entire plain of Piedmont as far as Milan, is extremely striking."

Fourthly, the Col de la Traversette fulfils the requirements of Varro's list of passes: it is situated between the Mont Genèvre and the Riviera and leads out of the Durance basin.

The result of these considerations is that the Col de Larche and the Mont Genèvre must be rejected as competitors for Hannibal's pass because they are too low and too easy and have no view of the plains of Lombardy. The same three objections apply to the Mont Cenis with the addition of a fourth that it does not lead out of the Durance basin, but that of the Isère. As for the Little St. Bernard which was so long the favourite for Hannibal's pass, it suffers not only from the same four objections as the Mont Cenis but also from two more: the distance by its route is too great from the "ascent towards the Alps" to the plains of Italy, and it does not lead into the country of the Taurini. In other words it has the least to be said for it of them all. The Col Clapier might be regarded as sufficiently high and dangerous on its descent and it has a view of the plains; but it leads out of the basin of the Isère and not that of the Durance.

The Col de la Traversette is the only one which satisfies all the requirements. That the valley of the Guil through which it is reached was in general use in early times is proved by the discovery of Roman inscriptions at

Les Escoyères in the valley of Queyras, and for the benefit of those who object that the Col de la Traversette is too difficult a pass for it to have been possible for Hannibal to have crossed it, elephants and all, it may be recalled that with the relatively primitive alpine experience and equipment available in 1860, John Ball described the ascent from the Italian side as lying "over steep slopes of débris or snow, according to the season, till the upper and steeper part of the ascent is reached, where it is necessary to keep to the track which mounts with tolerable rapidity, but without the slightest real difficulty, to the summit". The time required to walk all the way from Saluzzo to Montdauphin is given as 21½ hours. In 1907 the Col de la Traversette was the scene of an excursion described by Henri Ferrand to celebrate the re-opening of the tunnel. Ladies were present, and it cannot be contended that this route would have been beyond the powers of Hannibal's army, even if the ladies did not proceed higher than the tunnel.

The time of the year at which Hannibal reached the summit of the pass is deducible from Polybius's and Livy's statements that the setting of the Pleiades was approaching. Like many constellations the Pleiades, of course, set at some time every day, the time changing throughout the year. But the date at which the Pleiades rise at the same time as the sun was regarded by the ancients as marking the beginning of summer; while the date at which they set at the same time as the sun rises was regarded as heralding the onset of winter. As explained in Appendix C, the date when Hannibal reached the summit of the pass must have been the end of October.

The distance between the Col de Grimone and the Col de la Traversette is about 180 kilometres, and as Hannibal's vanguard covered it in nine days, the speed of his fastest troops in the Alps averaged 20 kilometres a day. This is at a faster rate than the 800 stadia (142 kilometres) which he marched "along the river" at 14 kilometres a day. This difference in speed may appear curious, but Polybius's account is quite specific as regards distances and the times taken to cover them. The total distance across the Alps, 1200 stadia (213 kilometres) took 15 days, but three of these were spent on the summit and the remaining two in reaching the plain, 40 kilometres from the Col de la Traversette.

Furthermore, the rate here given for Hannibal's alpine march compares favourably with Julius Caesar's march in 58 B.C. In his commentaries on the Gallic War,[77] Caesar described how he mobilised five legions in northern Italy and led them into Gaul. From Ocelum (Oulx) which is on the Italian side of Mont Genèvre, Caesar fought and defeated the Gauls who opposed his passage (Appian [78] called them Tricorii) and arrived at the frontier of the Vocontii in seven days. In fact Caesar's itinerary was almost the same as Hannibal's in the reverse direction, and the distance must have been equivalent. It is therefore not extravagant to claim that Hannibal covered in nine days a distance which Caesar marched in seven.

From the Col de la Traversette to the plains at Saluzzo the distance is about 40 kilometres, which would have occupied Hannibal's men on the fourteenth and fifteenth days. The total distance from the Col de Grimone to Saluzzo is 220 kilometres. This may be compared with Polybius's [16] estimate of 1200 stadia (or 213 kilometres) from "the ascent towards the Alps" to the plains of Italy.

Polybius's [79] statement that when Hannibal had

descended from the Alps he entered the territory of the
Insubres must be taken as a broad picture of events after

Monte Viso from Turin. The Col de la Traversette is in a notch
on the right of the skyline

the crossing of the Alps, because according to the geographer Ptolemy [80] the Insubres lived at Novara, Como,

Milan, and Pavia, and their territory nowhere touched
the Alps, from which they were separated by the Libici
and the Taurini. That this is the correct interpretation
of Polybius's text is clear from the sequel,[81] in which he
recorded that when Hannibal had rested his army after
its ordeal which made the men almost look like savages,
"he attempted to gain friendship and strike an alliance
with the Taurini who lived at the foot of the mountains,
pros tē parōreiā, were enemies of the Insubres [his allies],
and mistrusted the Carthaginians. But they rejected his
advances, so in three days he stormed their most important town." Livy must therefore have been right when he
wrote that "all were agreed" that Hannibal came down
from the Alps into the territory of the Taurini. The town
of *Augusta Taurinorum* is the present Turin.

A good deal of ridicule has been poured on Livy's [73]
description of Hannibal's method of removing a rock by
lighting a fire under it and then drenching it with
vinegar. The same story is also found in Timagenes and
in Appian. Such scepticism is unnecessary, for the prac-
tice is vouched for by several authorities. Pliny referred
to it twice:[82] "if fire has not disintegrated a rock, the
addition of water makes it split;" and:[83] "flints may be
cracked by fire and vinegar". This is confirmed by
Vitruvius:[84] "Stones which chisels and fire cannot break
are split and reduced to powder if first heated and then
drenched with vinegar." Dion Cassius [85] tells the same
story: "traitors destroyed a solidly built tower by means
of vinegar" which enabled Metellus to capture Eleuthera.
When the tunnel under the summit of the Col de la
Traversette was pierced in 1480, the expression "acetum"
appears in the licence granted by the Emperor Frederick
VI to the Marquis de Saluzzo to perform this operation.

Douglas Freshfield has related how he witnessed a similar event in the same region of the Alps. A farmer wished to remove a rock; he lit a bonfire round it and then drenched it with pails of liquid. Finally, it may be added that fire, water, and heavy hammers were used to split the Sarsen stones of Avebury.

The truth of Livy's story about the vinegar need therefore not be doubted. The more the accounts of ancient authors are studied in the light of modern knowledge, the greater is the aptness of Armandi's remark to the effect that recent naturalists and travellers have more than once vindicated the ancients from the scepticism that critics have shown towards their writings, and confirmed the accuracy of descriptions on which doubt had been thrown. To the story of the vinegar may be added the name of *Skaras*, and, as will shortly be seen, the size of the African war-elephant.

To revert to the vinegar episode, it remains to add that as trees were at hand to cut down and supply wood for the fire, the rock to be removed must have been below the summit of the pass.

X

HANNIBAL'S ALPS AND ELEPHANTS

WE HAVE NOW FOLLOWED HANNIBAL'S ROUTE FROM THE
Rhone to the Po. The identification of "the Island" with
the land between the Rhone and the Aygues is a certainty, and in consequence, so is that of the crossing of
the Rhone between Fourques and Arles. The delimita-
tion of the territories of the Tricastini, the Vocontii, and
the Tricorii is a certainty. The identification of "the
ascent towards the Alps" with the Col de Grimone is a
virtual certainty. That Hannibal's route lay through the
middle reaches of the Durance, and that his pass was the
Col de la Traversette are very high probabilities.

The route which I here advocate for Hannibal agrees
with every detail of Polybius's narrative including the
distances, with Strabo's and Varro's lists of passes, and
with every detail of Livy's narrative if allowance is made
for his calling the inhabitants of "the Island" Allobroges,
and for his placing the crossing of the Durance before the
first battle.

Although two thousand years away in time and a
thousand miles in space, these Alps, and elephants, have
a place in our literature and history which connects us
with Hannibal. In the Prologue of the Clerk's Tale
Chaucer referred to a mountain that was practically on
Hannibal's route:

> . . . And of Mount Vesulus in special,
> where as the Poo out of a welle smal
> Taketh his firste springyng and his sours.

And as for the elephants, did not Polyaenus [86] describe the battle of London? Caesar wanted to cross the Thames, which Cassivelaunus, King of the Britons, fought to prevent with many horsemen and chariots. But in his army Caesar had something which the Britons had never seen before: a huge elephant, protected with iron armour and bearing on its back a tower in which were archers and slingsmen, who were ordered to advance across the river. The Britons were terrified at the sight of such an outsize animal, against which horses were unavailing. For as in the case of the Greeks, horses bolted at the bare sight of an elephant. Nor could the Britons stand up to this armoured fighting animal possessed of fire-power and shooting arrows and sling-stones at them. With their horses and their chariots they turned and fled, and the Romans were able to cross the Thames without danger because their enemies took fright at one animal. An Elephant and Castle.

So it was with Hannibal's elephants; and although they appear to have had no castles, Polyaenus's description of Caesar and the Britons can be applied to Hannibal and the Gauls.

XI

EPILOGUE

To THE UTTER SURPRISE AND CONSTERNATION OF THE Romans, Hannibal and his army had crossed the Alps which they had never thought of guarding. In the words of Florus [87] who compared the Carthaginians with a thunderbolt, it burst its way through the middle of the Alps and descended on to Italy from those snows of fabulous height as if launched from the skies. The first storm broke with a mighty crash between the Po and the Ticino. The Roman army commanded by Publius Cornelius Scipio was put to flight and its wounded general would himself have fallen into the hands of the Carthaginians if his son had not saved him from death. This boy was the Scipio who was later to conquer Africa and take his title from the downfall of Carthage.

After the Ticino came the Trebbia, where the Second Punic War "wreaked its fury". On a cold and snowy day the Carthaginians warmed themselves at fires and rubbed their bodies with oil, and so the southerners from the lands of the sun were able to make use of the rigours of winter to beat the Roman army commanded by Tiberius Sempronius Longus. The weather was so inclement that all Hannibal's elephants died except one,[88] on which he afterwards rode.

Hannibal's third thunderbolt fell at Lake Trasimene where the Romans were commanded by Gaius Flaminius. The Carthaginians made use of a new ruse, for their cavalry, hidden by a mist from the lake and the marshy vegetation, unexpectedly fell on the rear of the

Romans, whose imprudent commander had been warned of imminent disaster by the settling of a swarm of bees on the standards, the difficulty in getting the eagles to advance, and a tremendous earthquake which occurred when the battle joined.

By this disaster all Etruria was lost to the Romans. Hannibal marched to the Adriatic coast and calmly re-organised his army both as regards tactics and weapons, using those which he had captured. When his men were rested he led them across the heart of Italy to Campania. There Quintus Fabius Maximus laid a trap for him. That Roman general was expecting Hannibal to march his army through the only pass across the Appenines available to him. But Hannibal had lighted torches tied to the horns of a number of cattle and drove them at night in another direction. The Romans mistook the cattle for the Carthaginians, while Hannibal's men were then able to slip through.

The fourth, and what might have been the final blow to the Roman state, was delivered at Cannae, a humble village of Apulia which came to notice from the magnitude of the Roman disaster, and acquired fame as the scene of the death of 60,000 men. On that field the great general, the terrain, the sky, and all nature conspired to bring about the annihilation of the unlucky Roman army. For Hannibal not only sent out bogus deserters, who subsequently fell on the rear of the combatants, but he took advantage of the nature of the terrain where the sun burned fiercely, there were clouds of dust, and the wind blew steadily from the east. He drew up his army in such a position that the Romans suffered from all these disadvantages while his men fought with the aid of the wind, the dust and the sun.

Hannibal's tactics at Cannae have never been surpassed nor even equalled. By withdrawing the centre of his army while its wings stood firm, the Romans were lured forward until they found themselves between the two jaws of the Carthaginian army, which closed in upon them like a vice and annihilated them. Of the Roman commanders, Lucius Aemilius Paullus was killed, and Gaius Terentius Varro fled from the field.

For Rome it was the blackest but also the finest hour. With every disaster the Roman determination to resist was strengthened, and in spite of his triumphs on battlefields Hannibal had already failed, for the Roman federation remained unshaken even if Capua did fall away. While the Roman federation existed, Hannibal could never be strong enough to capture Rome itself, for he had invaded Italy with less than 20,000 men, while Rome could call on three quarters of a million. Nevertheless, without a single friendly base, cut off from his home country by the seas which were under Roman control, Hannibal and his army were like a hostile clot roving about the body of Italy for fifteen years, during which he continued to shower defeats on one consular army after another. In addition to the disasters already mentioned, as the years went by the armies of Marcus Minutius Rufus, Tiberius Sempronius Gracchus, Marcus Centenius, Fulvius Centumalus, and Marcus Claudius Marcellus, were at one time or another defeated by Hannibal, and the Roman generals were killed.

Nine years after he had crossed the Alps, Hannibal called his brother Hasdrubal from Spain to him with his army, Hasdrubal came, but this time the Romans had wind of his coming. Two consular armies lay in wait for him and annihilated his army at the battle of Metaurus,

G

207 B.C. The first news that Hannibal received of the fate of his reinforcements was his brother's head, thrown into his camp by the Romans. "I see there the fate of Carthage," Hannibal mourned. This was the day which Horace in his Ode described as the first on which victory smiled on the Romans since the dreadful Carthaginians had crashed through the towns of Italy like a fire through a pine forest.

While Carthage failed to support Hannibal efficiently when he was in Italy, Carthage itself was presently invaded by the Romans in Africa, and Hannibal had to embark his army and return home to deal with a situation which he had always foreseen and tried to forestall. Even his military genius was unavailing, for at the battle of Zama in 202 B.C., Scipio Africanus was victorious, Carthage surrendered, and the Second Punic War came to an end.

It is difficult to give an idea of Hannibal's achievement in modern terms because the conditions were so different. Let us suppose however that during the battle of Britain in 1940 Rommel landed in Scotland with 20,000 men and 37 tanks, that he destroyed half a dozen British armies in as many battles, and roamed about the country from Edinburgh to Plymouth, ravaging and living on the land for fifteen years until, in 1955, having failed to detach the Scots and the Welsh from the English or to capture London, he re-embarked and sailed home to defend the Fatherland which Britain had at last succeeded in invading.

Where this parallel fails is of course the difference that Rommel would have found no semi-independent countries to side with him.

Just as Napoleon's name served as a bogey in British

nurseries to frighten naughty children, Hannibal's passed
into literature in the words *Hannibal ad portas*: Hannibal
is at the gates, but not so much to frighten children as to
galvanise the Roman people when threatened by mortal
danger.

At the conclusion of the Second Punic War the Romans
did not insist on the total destruction of Carthage. That
was reserved for the end of the Third Punic War, half a
century later. On this occasion, among the conditions of
peace enforced on Carthage was a measure of disarma-
ment whereby no elephants might be kept. The three
hundred elephant stables remained empty.

A few years later in 195 B.C., fearing that a demand for
the surrender of his person was about to be made by
Rome, Hannibal sailed away to Antiochus King of Syria
who must have been an attractive host to him because he
was soon engaged in fighting the Romans. Antiochus was
defeated at Magnesia in 190 B.C. and the Romans naturally demanded the surrender of Hannibal; but he sailed
away again to Crete.

This time, Hannibal ran the danger that the Cretans
knew how great was the sum of money which he had
brought with him. He countered this by filling a number
of large narrow-necked jars with lead, covered with gold
pieces at the top. These jars he deposited in the temple of
Diana, where the Cretans jealously mounted guard over
them, without molesting Hannibal. His real fortune he
placed inside some hollow bronze statues which he left
carelessly lying about his garden, so that when he wanted
to leave he was able to take his gold with him without the
Cretans' suspecting it.

Hannibal next took refuge with Prusias King of
Bithynia who was at war with Eumenes King of

Pergamum. This war gave Hannibal one last opportunity for showing his military genius. Prusias was defeated on land and transferred hostilities to the sea. Hannibal advised him to collect poisonous snakes, put them into earthenware jars, and throw them into the enemy's ships. The sailors of Pergamum began by jeering at such ridiculous tactics of fighting with pots instead of swords. But when the pots had broken and the Pergamene ships were crawling with snakes, the laugh was on the other side of their faces, and as Trogus Pompeius relates "they yielded the victory". This must have been one of the earliest known examples of biological warfare.

There followed yet another demand for the surrender of Hannibal whom the Romans pursued, as Plutarch said, "like a bird that had grown too old to fly and had lost its tail feathers".

He was sixty-four. Hannibal avoided his captors by taking poison, and as he did so he said: "Let us now put an end to the great anxiety of the Romans who have thought it too lengthy and too heavy a task to wait for the death of a hated old man." This was in 183 B.C., and the Romans breathed freely for the first time since that day thirty-five years before, when Hannibal crossed the Alps with his army and his elephants.

What can be said of the man himself? This was a question that Polybius also asked, but to which even he was unable to give anything like a complete answer; and it is a great pity that Plutarch only recorded a few anecdotes of him, for none better than he knew how to describe "a light occasion, a word, or some sport, which makes men's natural dispositions more plain than the famous battles won, wherein are slain ten thousand men". Nevertheless, some good stories have been recorded of Hannibal and they are all the more noteworthy because they were told by Romans, his bitter enemies.

First it is clear that Hannibal was a wit, as shown by his words at his death. There are other instances of this. One is related in Plutarch. When looking at the Roman army drawn up for battle at Cannae, his lieutenant Gisgo, like cousin Westmorland at Agincourt, bewailed the number of the enemy. Hannibal replied: "There is one thing, Gisgo, that you have not noticed, and that is that in all that great number of men opposite, there isn't a single one called Gisgo." They laughed so much that their mirth inspired the Carthaginian army with confidence.

After the fall of Carthage when Hannibal was in exile at Ephesus, Cicero relates that he attended a lecture by Phormio on the duties of army commanders. When Hannibal was asked what he thought of it, he replied: "I have seen many an old fool during my life, but this one beats them all." Also at Ephesus there took place the interview recorded by Livy and Plutarch between Hannibal and his old enemy the victor of Zama, Scipio Africanus. They talked about great army commanders. Scipio asked who Hannibal thought was the greatest general.

"Alexander the Great," replied Hannibal.

"Who do you put next?" asked Scipio.

"Pyrrhus."

"Who do you put third?"

"Myself."

Scipio laughed and continued: "What would you have said if you had defeated me?"

"I should have regarded myself as the greatest general of all." Scipio appreciated the compliment. But although he did not defeat Scipio, many will feel that Hannibal

deserves pride of place before Alexander who enjoyed
unlimited resources and had no great opponent except
Memnon, whereas Hannibal was unsupported and pitted
against great generals.

There could also be cynicism in Hannibal's wit. When
Antiochus proudly showed him the great battle array
with which he was about to try conclusions with the
Romans, Hannibal replied: "Yes, it will be enough for
the Romans, however greedy they may be." In much the
same vein two thousand years later, Wellington said of
Blücher's position at Ligny: "He will get damnably
mauled."

Witty men are usually ingenious, and several examples
have already been given of Hannibal's resourcefulness.
His ruses were so numerous and his stratagems so subtle
that the Romans felt constantly insecure. He became the
embodiment of what the Romans called "Punic faith", by
which they meant treacherousness. When they did the
same thing, it was of course no longer treachery. Even
Albion has been called perfidious.

The Romans must have thought of Hannibal what an
Austrian general once said of Napoleon: "We have to
deal with a young man who is at one moment on our
front, next on our flank, and then in our rear. One cannot
tell how to post oneself. This manner of making war is
insufferable. He breaks all the rules."

Again like Napoleon who insisted that his murder of
the Duc d'Enghien was a crime not a blunder, Hannibal
was not afraid of the truth even if told against himself.
When Quintus Fabius Maximus recaptured Tarentum,
Hannibal remarked: "So the Romans also have a Hannibal. They have taken Tarentum as we did," that is, by
treachery.

Some utterances of Hannibal which Plutarch recorded often show that verbal elegance which Lord Chesterfield called the "turn". It involves the happy repetition of a word, often with a deft antithesis. So it is related that Hannibal feared Fabius Maximus as a schoolmaster but regarded Marcellus as an antagonist, for the former prevented him from doing any mischief while the latter might make him suffer it. As for Marcellus, Hannibal said that he "is the only general who when victorious allows the enemy no rest, and when defeated takes none himself"

There was chivalry in Hannibal's character, for after the battles in which Lucius Aemilius Paullus, Tiberius Sempronius Gracchus, and Marcus Claudius Marcellus were killed, he sought out their bodies from among the piles of dead and gave them ceremonial burial. Marcellus's ashes he returned to his son in a silver urn. He spared Fabius's farm from devastation. The Romans said that he did this in order that they should suspect Fabius's loyalty.

Of Hannibal's conduct to women, Justin recorded that he behaved with such perfect propriety to his female captives that it was hard to believe that he was born in Africa. In spite of Appian who said that during one winter in Lucania Hannibal "abandoned himself to unaccustomed luxury and the delights of love", a remark which appears to have been nothing but Roman propaganda to discredit him, Hannibal seems to have been constantly faithful to his wife Imilce. She came from Castulo, a town on the Guadalquivir in Spain, which according to Silius Italicus was founded by Imilce's ancestor Castalius, a native of Delphi. Mrs. Hannibal would therefore have been of Greek descent.

Hannibal must have married Imilce about 220 B.C., and their son was born during the siege of Saguntum. Silius Italicus's poem relates Imilce's plea to Hannibal to let her accompany him on his march across the Alps: "Does our union and our nuptial joys make you think that I, your wife, would fail to climb the frozen mountains with you? Have faith in a woman's hardihood."

Like that other great campaigner in Spain, Wellington, Hannibal believed that an army on active service was no place for wives, and he took leave of Imilce with an exhortation to bring up their son, like himself, to be a hope of Carthage and the dread of Rome. They must have been parted for sixteen years. Even allowing for Silius Italicus's poetic licence, there is nothing in this episode contrary to what is known of Hannibal's character.

At the same time, Hannibal was accused during his life of great cruelty and great avarice, and both may have been true, the former being chiefly the reproach of the Romans, the latter of the Carthaginians. It must be said, however, that when he was planning to march across the Alps, the difficulties of supply appeared to be so formidable to one of his officers called Monomachus that he could see no solution of the problem unless the soldiers were trained to become cannibals. Polybius recorded that Hannibal appreciated the value of this suggestion but could not bring himself to consider it. He added that the cruelties attributed to Hannibal may have been really the work of Monomachus.

Cornelius Nepos has related that in spite of his warlike career, Hannibal had nevertheless found time to be a man of letters, and had written books in Greek. Among these was one addressed to the Rhodians on the deeds of Gnaeus Manlius Vulso in Asia. What would one not give to know if Hannibal described his own campaigns?

Perhaps the clearest light on Hannibal's character is shown by the fact that although he maintained his army permanently mobilised on active service in enemy territory for fifteen unbroken years, and although the men were Africans, Spaniards, Balearic Islanders, Ligurians, Gauls, Phoenicians, Italians, and Greeks, none of whom had anything in common, they never murmured against him nor showed any dissensions between themselves. Hannibal's power of leadership and man-management must have been unsurpassed.

On one occasion in Spain when a column of his cavalry was cut off by a river, he swam across it alone and encouraged his men after him. Soldiers would do anything for a man who, as Livy relates, was fearless in danger, indefatigable, undeterred by heat or cold, abstemious in food and drink, was content to sleep on the ground between the sentries and the outposts, covered only with a cloak, and dressed in the same way as his men. What distinguished him, however, was the excellence and care of his weapons and his horses, of which he was very fond, and his horsemanship. It was surely not by accident that some coins struck during his period of power in Spain show a magnificent charger on the reverse.

There are many instances of the care which he took of his animals. The method by which the elephants were conveyed across the Rhone shows that he understood them; and when after the hardships of the crossing of the Alps and the campaign in Northern Italy his cavalry horses were in poor condition and developed hunger-mange, he cured them by bathing them in "old wine", as Polybius [89] relates. There can hardly have been an old soldier's trick that Hannibal did not know.

Hannibal's appearance is possibly shown on the obverse of the silver hexadrachm pieces struck at Carthagena at about the time of his election as General in 221 B.C. Officially, this head may be taken to represent Melcarth, the Carthaginian equivalent of Hercules; but it is probable that Hannibal was the model for this "beardless Hercules", while his father Hamilcar Barca served as the model for the earlier bearded effigy of the god. Hamilcar's name means "Son of Melcarth". There is a strong similarity between the features of these coins which would be explained by the family connexion. Hannibal appears with a very strong forehead, a bright and open expression, not without a sense of humour.

For the rest, nothing more is known about Hannibal, but there is still this to be said. He was beaten by Scipio Africanus, and Carthage was destroyed by Rome. Rome certainly made good her victory, and nobody would dream of admitting Carthage to comparison with her as regards their relative contributions to civilisation. And yet Hannibal has somehow defeated his conquerors in the corridors of time, and commands a sympathy which is not accorded to Scipio. In spite of his innumerable other adventures and prowesses, I am not sure that it was not his outstanding passage of the Alps that attracted peoples' fancies and laid the basis of Hannibal's popularity. It has certainly led to a lot of thought and work to try to discover the way which he went on that wonderful march which both opened and set the seal on his career. I like to think that I know which way that was, but of course I may be wrong. That is why I have given references to the more important passages in the classical texts, so that any reader who fancies himself at all as a detective can consult them, in the originals or in translations, and solve the problem of Hannibal's route across the Alps for himself.

APPENDIX A

THE ELEPHANT OF MAILLANE

WHEN DIGGING IN HIS CELLAR ABOUT THE YEAR 1777, M. Barthélémy Daillan, an inhabitant of Maillane, found a copper medallion and the skeleton of an elephant 12 feet long. It was at first thought to be the remains of a human giant, but it was recognised as an elephant when two of its molar teeth were shown to Claude-François Achard, who recorded the find in his *Description Historique de la Provence*, published in 1788. M. Daillan fixed the copper medallion on to the handle of his pick to embellish it. The bones were broken in getting them out, but in 1824 the Comte de Villeneuve recorded in his *Statistique du Departement des Bouches du Rhone* that the widowed Mme Daillan still possessed one of the molar teeth, and that M. Toulousan had seen a piece of the femur in a farm near Saint-Etienne-du-Grès and confirmed that it was that of an elephant. The Comte de Villeneuve concluded that the most probable explanation of the find was that the skeleton belonged to one of Hannibal's elephants that became a casualty after the crossing of the Rhone.

This explanation is perfectly possible, for Maillane lies on the route from Arles to "the Island", and if it could be confirmed it would prove that Hannibal crossed the Rhone in this neighbourhood.

The only other reference to this find was made by Theodore Andreas Cook in his *Old Provence* where the nature of the elephant is specified as African. A glance at the molar teeth would settle this point instantly, but all attempts to trace them have failed. In the absence of any confirmatory evidence by Mr. Cook it is to be feared that his identification of the elephant as African may have been based on the Comte de Villeneuve's supposition that it had belonged to Hannibal; and this in turn rests on the assumption that Hannibal's elephants were African.

The identification of the nature of Hannibal's elephants is a matter of unexpected complexity and depends

African elephants on reverse of Carthaginian coins, 220 B.C.

in part on the evidence supplied by coins. The beautiful issue of Carthaginian coins in Spain which were practically contemporary with Hannibal's campaign bear on the reverse side the image of an unmistakable African elephant. It can be distinguished from an Indian elephant by the following features:

1. The back shows a concave dip between a hump over the shoulders and another hump over the hind quarters, whereas the Indian elephant's back is an unbroken convex dome;

2. The hind quarters are almost flat instead of projecting backwards at a fairly sharp angle as in the Indian elephant;

3. The head is carried high instead of in the low position characteristic in the Indian elephant;

4. The forehead is flat instead of showing the Indian elephant's concave profile;

5. The ear is very large instead of small;

6. The trunk is marked by repeated transverse ridges instead of being smooth;

7. The tip of the trunk has two "fingers" instead of the single one at the front edge in the Indian elephant;

8. The upper part of the hind leg is masked by a fold

Indian elephant on reverse of Etrurian coin, 217 B.C.

of skin of the flank, whereas in the Indian elephant the outside of the hind leg is distinctly visible right up to the groin.

All these features can be clearly seen on the Carthaginian coins and prove beyond a doubt that Hannibal used African elephants.

The proportions of the elephant and its rider on the Carthaginian coins show that the elephant was about 8 feet high. As Sir William Gowers has shown, the African elephants used by the Egyptian Pharaohs and by the Carthaginians were of the small forest type, variety *cyclotis*, standing about 8 feet high at the shoulder, and not of the large African bush elephant race which reaches 11 feet. The latter is larger than the Indian elephant, but the Indian is larger than the African forest elephant. The ancient authors Polybius, Ctesias and Philostratos, were perfectly correct when they described the African war-elephant as being no match for the Indian, and modern critics who have tried to ridicule the ancients have only succeeded in demonstrating their own ignorance of zoology.

The Carthaginians' African elephants were obtained from the foot of the Atlas mountains and the coast of Morocco where Hanno [90] saw them about 500 B.C., Herodotus described them, and Hasdrubal Gisgo [91] was sent to find some in 205 B.C. Suetonius Paulinus [92] surveyed the area in A.D. 47 and particularly the forested valley of the Guir with its wild animals including the elephant. Its disappearance forms part of an Arab legend, concerning which Mr. Ritchie Calder was recently shown a manuscript at the tomb of Sidi Tayeb. This saint was bitten by a snake and, as he was dying, called on the animals in the name of Allah to leave the forest of Guir, which they did six days later. In Pliny's time elephants were plentiful around Ghadames, south of Tunisia.[93] Today the forest elephant in the west of Africa does not extend farther north than Senegal.

The Pharaohs' African elephants were obtained from the shores of the Red Sea and Eritrea where forest elephants were still living at the time of Napier's expedition to Magdala in 1868. Today in East Africa they do not extend farther north than the areas bordering the Nile in the Sudan.

Although there is no doubt that the Carthaginians

used African elephants, the question arises whether they might not have had Indian elephants as well. Some authorities have assumed that they did, simply because Polybius [94] referred to the drivers of the Carthaginians' elephants as *indoi*. But this name must be based on the fact that ever since war-elephants were first encountered in Porus's army by Alexander the Great at the battle of the Hydaspes in 326 B.C., Indian trainers and drivers were regarded as the experts. When the Pharaohs began to use African elephants, they imported Indian trainers, and the word *indos* must have come to mean an elephant-driver. The dress of the driver of the elephant on the Carthaginian coins suggests that he was African.

It might be imagined that as India and Carthage were at opposite ends of the known world, it would not have been possible for the Carthaginians to obtain Indian elephants, but this is not so. After the death of Alexander the Great, his successors became so impressed with the prestige and power conferred by the possession of these new armoured fighting animals that they left no stone unturned to acquire elephants. The Ptolemies managed to get some in repeated wars against the rulers of Syria, and they were all Indian elephants. Ptolemy I probably captured some from Perdiccas in 321 B.C. when the latter invaded Egypt with a force of elephants and was defeated.

Nine years later Ptolemy captured all Demetrius's forty-three elephants at Gaza, and Indian elephants are depicted on a gold stater minted about 300 B.C. In the third Syrian war, which was fought between 246 and 241, Ptolemy III defeated Seleucus and captured more Indian elephants.

During this period the relations between Egypt and Carthage were close and friendly, and it is known that

H

Ptolemy II lent Carthage large sums of money during the first Punic War. It is necessary to believe that Egypt also sent elephants, including Indian elephants, to Carthage, because of the evidence provided by a remarkable coin from Etruria. This coin bears on the obverse an obvious African negro's head, and on the reverse an equally obvious Indian elephant, as may be seen by comparing it with the African.

The Chiana valley of Etruria is far removed from the parts of Italy through which Pyrrhus passed with his Indian elephants in 279 B.C., but it is on the line of Hannibal's march to Lake Trasimene after he had crossed the Alps. It is known from Polybius that after the battle of the Trebbia all Hannibal's elephants died except one on which he himself rode across the Apennines. It is also known from Pliny[95] that Cato, no friend of Carthage, recorded that the elephant which fought most bravely in the Punic Wars was called *Surus*. Surus means "the Syrian", and Syria was where the Ptolemy's Indian elephants came from. It is therefore almost certain, as Sir William Gowers and Dr. H. H. Scullard have shown, that Hannibal's elephants included at least one Indian. It is also very possible that Hannibal's surviving elephant, *Surus*, is depicted on the Etrurian coins.

It is a long way back from the great events of ancient history to the little village of Maillane, but their import is that as Hannibal possessed Indian as well as African elephants, the attribution to Hannibal of the elephant of Maillane would not be established even if it were proved that it was African. This is all the more the case because Hannibal was not the only general to lead elephants through Provence. When the Romans conquered Provence in 121 B.C., they sent Domitius and

Fabius to show the flag with elephants in a military
parade described by Suetonius.[96] These elephants were
certainly African and were probably supplied by the
King of Mauretania, Micipsa, whose father Masinissa
had frequently furnished elephants to Rome.

Suspicious and critical minds may ask why the elephant of Maillane might not have been the remains of
the extinct meridional elephant or those of a mammoth,
both inhabitants of France during the Ice Ages, preserved as fossils in the river terraces of the Rhone. The
answer is the copper medallion which was found with
it, indicating that the elephant was deliberately buried.
The only evidence which might have established a connexion between the Maillane elephant and Hannibal
was the effigy or inscription on that medallion which
went to ornament the handle of Monsieur Barthélémy
Daillan's pick. Unless that is found it will never be known
if the Maillane elephant belonged to Hannibal.

APPENDIX B

THE BOGUS ELEPHANT OF LA BÂTIE-NEUVE

THE MAGAZINE *ZOO LIFE* IN ITS SUMMER ISSUE FOR 1950, contained an article on the "King of the Kraals" by James E. Carver with numerous references to Hannibal's elephants on his march across the Alps. Some of these references are to stories the validity of which is doubtful, such as the statement that the elephants were protected by hanging plates and bore archers in towers on their backs. There is a fragment in Suidas, very doubtfully attributed to Polybius, where mention is made of armour, but the whole passage makes very little sense, and as Dr. H. H. Scullard has pointed out, the general impression made by Polybius's accounts of battles suggests that Hannibal's elephants bore no towers. It is also difficult to see where Mr. Carver finds authority for his statement that "few that set out with Hannibal reached Italy. For some were slaughtered before the mountains were crossed, others fell over the precipices, and yet more were frozen to death." Neither Polybius nor Livy refers to any casualties suffered by the elephants.

Much more sensational however is Mr. Carver's paragraph which states that "A fascinating discovery was made about ten years back by a French archaeologist, Dr. Laurent Bernard, near the village of Avançon, in the Durance valley. Looking for relics of the Iron Age, he came upon tusks of African elephants, and the spot is thought to be one of the places where Hannibal killed some of his beasts."

Hannibal can of course have had no reason whatever to slaughter any of his precious elephants in the fertile Durance valley, where the food supply cannot have occasioned any difficulties at all. This story can be traced to the fantastic articles published in 1938 by *L'Illustration* and *Le Petit Dauphinois*, which were so misleading as to be absurd. They referred to the discovery on 15 June 1938 of a late Stone Age burial in a mound at La Bâtie-Neuve in the Départment des Hautes Alpes. It was said to contain ivory tusks, which, in the minds of the journalists concerned, was sufficient to associate the whole site with Hannibal. But as M. Georges de Manteyer informed me on 23 February 1946, the objects supposed to be elephants' tusks were really bones of the aurochs, *Bos primigenius*, associated with flint implements and beads surrounding a human skeleton without any metallic remains whatever. The relics have, of course, nothing at all to do with Hannibal whom they antedate by two thousand years, and it is only a coincidence that they should lie on what is believed to be his line of march.

APPENDIX C

THE SETTING OF THE PLEIADES

THE PLEIADES OF COURSE SET AT SOME TIME EVERY DAY, whether observable by man or not. During the summer they may be observed in the sky during the night, but in the morning the sun rises and they become invisible before they have set. However, since the stars appear to gain on the sun by about 4 minutes of time each day, which means that every day they set about 4 minutes earlier than the day before, the day eventually arrives some time in winter when the Pleiades set at the same moment as the sun rises.

In latitude 45° N. at sea level, with a clear horizon, allowing 35 minutes of arc for refraction by the earth's atmosphere, and taking the centre of the Pleiades as having a declination of 24° 02′ N. and a right ascension of 3 hr. 43 m. 44 sec., the setting of the Pleiades takes place at sunrise on 24th November, 1954.

But although the Pleiades are setting at sunrise on this date, they cannot of course be seen to be setting because daylight obscures them. In order to be seen setting, the Pleiades must gain further on the sun, so as to set sometime before dawn. The last moment before dawn at which this constellation, which is not a very bright one, could reasonably be expected to be visible would be about the moment of "nautical twilight", when the sun is yet 12 degrees below the horizon and in the words of the Nautical Almanac: "General outlines will still be visible, although the horizon cannot be distinguished." The first

100

day when this is observable is the date of the "setting of the Pleiades" as understood by the ancients, a date of agricultural importance to them which was regarded as marking the onset of winter. We know this from Lucius Junius Moderatus Columella,[97] a farmer who wrote in the 1st century A.D. The date on which, in 1954, the Pleiades set at the moment of nautical twilight is the 8th December. This seems to be the best estimate that can be made of the "setting of the Pleiades" as understood by the ancients, and applied to the present day.

It now remains to correct these dates so as to arrive at the corresponding dates in 218 B.C. The difference is due to the precession of the equinoxes. The point at which the plane of the earth's revolution round the sun (the ecliptic) intersects the equator, moves backward on the ecliptic by approximately 50·03 seconds of arc each year. Expressed in degrees that is equal to 50·03 divided by 3600 (the number of seconds in a degree), or 0·01389 degree each year. To convert this angular measurement into a measurement of time in days, this figure must be divided by 360 (the number of degrees in a circle) and multiplied by 365·25 (the number of days roughly in the year), which gives 0·01409 days each year. Hannibal's date, 218 B.C., was 2172 years before 1954, and in that time the precession of the equinoxes has made a difference of 0·01409 × 2172, or 30·6 days in the date when the Pleiades set at the time when the sun rises.

Thirty and a half days before 24 November gives 24 October as the date when the Pleiades actually set at sunrise in 218 B.C., but they would be invisible. Thirty and a half days before 8 December gives 7 November as the earliest date for the visible "setting of the Pleiades" in 218 B.C.

The date of 24 October for the actual setting of the Pleiades in 218 B.C., is very close to that of 25 October proposed by Professor Charles Pritchard for J. L. Strachan-Davidson, and to that of 26 October which was worked out by Neville Maskelyne, Astronomer Royal, for General Robert Melville. It is also in agreement with the bracket of dates given by Columella [97] in the 1st century A.D., namely between 20 and 28 October.

Columella's dates were reckoned according to the Julian calendar which was instituted in 45 B.C. By the 1st century A.D. its imperfections had not yet had time to make an error equivalent to a day in the difference between the civil year and the solar year. Columella's dates may therefore be taken as equivalent to the same dates as expressed in the Gregorian calendar today. They are, however, the dates of the astronomical but invisible setting of the Pleiades, and it is not clear how Columella arrived at them, nor of what use they would have been to farmers if they could not see them.

The date of 7 November for the earliest visible setting of the Pleiades is in close agreement with that of 9 November proposed by Strachan-Davidson as a result of applying Ptolemy's [98] definition of the "aspects" of stars with reference to the sun. Strachan-Davidson has also quoted Geminus (1st century B.C.) as stating that the setting of the Pleiades was put on 7 November by Euctemon (5th century B.C.), 8 November by Callippus (4th century B.C.) and 11 November by Eudoxus (4th century B.C.).

Pliny,[99] writing in the 1st century A.D. said that "about 44 days after the autumn equinox, the Setting of the Pleiades heralds the onset of winter which normally falls about 11 November". But the equinox is 23 September, and 44 days after this date is 6 November. Pliny's dates for the Setting of the Pleiades therefore straddle those of the other classical authors.

From all these results it is clear that the setting of the Pleiades in Polybius's and Livy's accounts was a date about 7 November, and as this date was approaching, Hannibal must have reached the summit of his pass about the end of October.

APPENDIX D

THE CLIMATE IN 218 B.C.

THERE ARE FOUR INDEPENDENT WAYS IN WHICH AN estimate can be obtained of the state of the climate in 218 B.C. The first is based on the study of glaciers, since the size and extension of glaciers is dependent on a general, though possibly only slight, reduction in world temperature. At the places to which glaciers extend, they pile up the boulders which they have carried down from the mountains to form terminal moraines which can be recognised as mounds and ridges in the valleys. From a study of these in the Alps, H. Kinzl has concluded that since the last phases of the Ice Age a few thousand years ago, the glaciers never advanced again as much as they did in the 17th and 19th centuries. This means that the present conditions of the glaciers is not a diminished relic of their extension in the last Ice Age, but a relic of their recent maximum. Before the 17th century it is certain that they were, indeed, much smaller than they are now. This is known from the fact that in the Middle Ages some alpine passes such as the St. Theodul were easily crossed on horseback, whereas now they involve crossing glaciers and snow-fields.

Now that the glaciers are retreating, they are constantly uncovering trunks of trees which are the remains of forests destroyed by the glacial advances of the 17th century. I have myself obtained and placed in the Natural History Museum a large piece of the trunk of *Pinus cembra* from the side of the Lower Grindelwald

Glacier at a height of 1700 metres, where there are no trees now. In the Alps of Piedmont, U. Monterin found a large trunk of *Picea excelsa* uncovered by a glacier at a height of over 2250 metres. It is also known that a thousand years ago, Greenland was "green", during a period of optimum warm temperature.

It is of course difficult to equate these glacial phenomena with the chronology of classical history, but Strabo [100] quoted Polybius as saying that in the country of the Taurisci among the Noric Alps, there were in his time gold mines worked with great profit. These mines in the High Tauern are well known, in the group of mountains appropriately called the Goldberg, and they were intensively worked in the Middle Ages. In the 17th century, however, extensions of the glaciers covered the adits to some of these mines, and they have not been exploited since then. This would indicate that in the 2nd century B.C. the temperature was not colder than it is now.

The second method of estimating past climate is by means of the height above sea-level of the tree-line, measured in places where it has not been affected either by the advance of glaciers or by human agencies such as the pasturing of animals and the direct use of wood for fuel. U. Monterin has provided evidence from many sources that show that in Northern Italy the tree-line is today at least 1000 feet lower than it has been. The question of course is, at what time was the tree-line higher, and to this it is very difficult to supply an objective answer. Nevertheless, it is a fact that a Roman author, Virgil,[76] refers to Monte Viso as *Vesulus pinifer*: pine-clad Viso. It bears no pine forests round its summit today.

The third method makes use of the analysis of pollen-grains found in the peat-bogs, since it reveals the identity of the prevalent trees, and the various species of trees have different optimum climates. As summarised by H. Godwin and L. von Post, these indicate temperature maxima at A.D. 1200 and 550 B.C.

Levels are found where there is a lower layer of well-humified peat formed under drier and perhaps warmer conditions, underlying a layer formed under wetter and cooler conditions.

In the Lower Rhone valley, J. Gourc has shown that after a period of warm climate characterised by preval-ence of the nut-tree *Corylus*, there followed a cooler period similar to that of the present day, when birch, beech, and alder flourished. On the other side of the Alps, in Northern Italy, P. Keller has found similar conditions.

It is clear that in Hannibal's time, 218 B.C., the climate was not as warm as during the temperature maximum of 550 B.C., but that does not mean that it was worse than it is now. This is where the fourth method of estimating past climate is especially useful. It is based on the conditions under which sediments were deposited at the bottom of the Atlantic Ocean. J. D. H. Wiseman's researches in this field have shown that the quantity of calcium carbonate deposited is dependent on the tem-perature at the surface. In 550 B.C. the rate was 1·0 milli-grams of calcium carbonate per square centimetre per year, as compared with 0·9 milligrams today, which means that the temperature in 550 B.C. was on average 1 or 2 degrees higher than now. These results are con-firmed by C. D. Ovey's observations on the relative pre-ponderance in the deposits of shells of Foraminifera belonging to tropical and to arctic species. The values

for the temperature in 218 B.C. were intermediate
between those of 550 B.C. and today.

From all these results it may safely be concluded that
the climate in Hannibal's time was no colder than it is
now, and therefore that the snow-line was then no lower.
It follows therefore that the pass which Hannibal crossed
and where he found snow of the previous year in large
quantities must have been high.

APPENDIX E

WHERE OTHERS HAVE MADE HANNIBAL GO

THE NUMBER OF AUTHORS WHO HAVE TRIED TO SOLVE the puzzle of Hannibal's route runs into hundreds. I have selected thirty for analysis here. In the following table, 1 is the place of crossing the Rhone, 2 the river identified as *Skaras* and *Arar*, 3 the place of the beginning of the ascent, 4 the site of the enemy's town, 5 the line of march, and 6 the watershed pass into Italy. Not all these six places were identified by each author.

Josias Simler, 1574. 2 Saone, 6 Mont Cenis or Mont Genèvre.

Edward Gibbon, 1763. 2 Isère, 6 Mont Genèvre.

C. Denina, 1792. 2 Isère, 6 Col de la Traversette.

J. Whittaker, 1794. 1 Loriol, 2 Saone, 3 Martigny, 4 Sembrancher, 5 Lyon–St. Genis–Seyssel–Geneva–Martigny–Val de Bagnes, 6 Grand St. Bernard.

Napoleon, 1816. 1 Roquemaure, 6 Mont Cenis.

J. A. de Luc, 1818. 1 Roquemaure, 2 Isère, 3 Mont du Chat, 4 Léminc, 5 Vienne–St. Genis–Le Bourget–Chambéry-Tarentaise, 6 Petit St. Bernard.

Letronne, 1819. 1 Roquemaure, 2 Isère, 3 St. Bonnet, 5 Col Bayard–Gap–Briançon, 6 Mont Genèvre.

Ladoucette, 1820. 2 Isère, 6 Mont Genèvre.

G. L. Wickham and J. A. Cramer, 1820. 1 Roquemaure, 2 Isère, 3 Mont du Chat, 4 Le Bourget, 5 Bourgoin-Chambéry-Tarentaise, 6 Petit St. Bernard.

Fortia d'Urban, 1821. 1 Roquemaure, 2 Aygues, 3 Mont-saléon, 4 Gap, 5 Embrun–Briançon, 6 Mont Genèvre.

108

J. L. Larauza, 1826. 1 Roquemaure, 2 Isère, 3 Mont-mélian, 4 St. Georges d'Urtière, 5 Grenoble–Mauri-enne, 6 Mont Cenis.

Cambridge, Anonymous, 1830. 1 Tarascon, 2 Isère, 3 St. Bonnet, 4 La Bréole, 5 Col Bayard–Gap–Barcelon-nette–Col de Vars–Chateau Queyras, 6 Col de la Traversette.

H. L. Long, 1831. 1 Tarascon, 2 Isère, 3 Montmélian, 4 Grenoble, 5 Tarentaise, 6 Petit St. Bernard.

R. Ellis, 1853. 1 Tarascon, 2 Isère, 3 Le Fay, 4 Allevard, 5 Aiguebelle–Maurienne, 6 Petite Mont Cenis.

W. J. Law, 1866. 1 Roquemaure, 2 Isère, 3 Mont du Chat, 4 Bordeau, 5 Vienne–Bourgoin–Chambéry–Tarentaise, 6 Petit St. Bernard.

Colonel Hennebert, 1878. 1 Roquemaure, 2 Isère, 3 St. Bonnet, 4 Grenoble, 5 Drac–Col de la Pioly-Embrun, 6 Mont Genèvre.

Colonel Perrin, 1887. 1 Pont St. Esprit, 2 Isère, 3 Mont de l'Epine, 4 Léminc, 5 Chambéry–Maurienne, 6 Col Clapier.

Dr. Ollivier, 1889. 1 Roquemaure, 2 Isère, 3 Col de Cabre, 4 Le Lauzet, 5 Rousset–La Bréole–Barcelon-nette, 6 Col de Roure.

T. Montanari, 1890. 1 Tarascon [*Rhodanos* = Durance], 2 Verdon, 5 Sisteron–Gap–Embrun, 6 Col de l'Echelle.

T. A. Dodge, 1891. 1 Roquemaure, 2 Isère, 3 Mont du Chat, 5 Vienne–Chambéry–Tarentaise, 6 Petit St. Bernard.

J. Fuchs, 1897. 1 Roquemaure, 2 Isère, 5 Grenoble–Col Bayard–Embrun, 6 Mont Genèvre.

W. H. Bullock Hall, 1898. 1 Roquemaure, 2 Isère, 5 Grenoble–Maurienne, 6 Mont Cenis.

W. Osiander, 1900. 1 Pont St. Esprit, 2 Isère, 3 Mont-mélian, 4 St. Jean de Maurienne, 5 Maurienne, 6 Mont Cenis.

P. Azan, 1902. 1 Lardoise, 2 Isère, 3 Col de Cucheron, 4 St. Alban, 5 Grésivaudan–Maurienne, 6 Col Clapier.

J. Colin, 1904. 1 Fourques, 2 Durance, 3 Bec d'Echaillon, 4 Grenoble, 5 Grésivaudan–Col de Cucheron-Maurienne, 6 Col Clapier.

Spenser Wilkinson, 1911. 1 Fourques, 2 Sorgues, 3 Bec d'Echaillon, 4 Grenoble, 5 Grésivaudan–Col de Cucheron–Maurienne, 6 Col Clapier.

D. W. Freshfield, 1914. 1 Roquemaure, 2 Isère, 3 St. Bonnet, 4 Gap, 5 Drac–Col Bayard–Guillestre-Col du Vars–Barcelonnette, 6 Col de Larche.

H. Ferrand, 1925. 1 Fourques, 2 Sorgues, 3 Bec d'Echaillon, 4 Grenoble, 5 Grésivaudan–Maurienne, 6 Col Clapier.

C. Torr, 1925. 1 Tarascon, 2 Durance, 3 Mirabeau, 4 Ville-Vieille, 5 Sisteron–Montdauphin–Guillestre-Chateau Queyras, 6 Col de la Traversette.

A. R. Bonus, 1925. 5 Col de Lautaret–Col de Malrif, 6 Col de Malaure.

G. de Manteyer, 1944. 1 Lardoise, 2 Isère, 3 Col de Grimone, 5 Col de Rognon–Mens–Col de Manse-Embrun–Barcelonnette, 6 Col de Marie.

BIBLIOGRAPHY

(In the following list of references are included only those works which have been of direct assistance to the present study. No attempt has been made to record the vast literature on the problem of Hannibal's route)

ABAUZIT, F. *Œuvres diverses.* Genève, 1770.

ARMANDI, P. *Histoire militaire des éléphants.* Paris, 1843.

BALL, JOHN. *Alpine Guides. South Western Alps,* p. 24. London, 1873.

CALDER, RITCHIE. "Hannibal and his Elephants," *New Statesman,* May, 6, 1950.

CLOUDSLEY-THOMPSON, J. L. "The Lucanian Cows," *School Science Review,* No. 128, 1954, p. 66.

CLOUZOT, ETIENNE. "Pouillés des Provinces d'Aix, d'Arles, et d'Embrun," *Recueil des Historiens de la France.* Paris, 1923.

—— "Pouillés des Provinces de Besançon, de Tarentaise, et de Vienne," *Ibid.* Paris, 1940.

COLIN, J. *Annibal en Gaule.* Paris, 1904.

DESJARDINS, ERNEST. *Géographie historique et administrative de la Gaule romaine.* Paris, 1876–93.

FORBES, JAMES DAVID. *Life and Letters,* p. 250. London, 1873.

FRESHFIELD, D. *Hannibal Once More.* London, 1914.

GOURG, J. "La Méthode pollen-analytique et son application à l'étude des temps Post-Glaciaires. Analyse du Marais des Echets (Ain). Les études rhodaniennes," *Revue de Géographie Régionale,* 12, pp. 63–81. Lyon, 1936.

GOWERS, SIR WILLIAM. "African Elephants and Ancient Authors," *African Affairs,* 173–9. London, July 1948.

—— and SCULLARD, H. H. "Hannibal's Elephants Again," *Numismatic Chronicle,* 6th Series, 10, 1950, pp. 271–83.

HATTO, A. T. "The Elephants in the Strasburg Alexander." *London Mediaeval Studies,* 1, 1948, pp. 399–429.

HOLDER, A. T. *Altkeltischer Sprachschatz,* 9th Part, col. 16. Leipzig, 1896–1904.

JOANNE, P. *Dictionnaire géographique de la France,* 3, p. 1436. Paris, 1894.

I   111

112   BIBLIOGRAPHY

KELLER, P. "Die Postglaziale Entwicklungsgeschichte der Wälder von Norditalien," *Veröffentlichungen des Geobotanischen Institutes Rübel in Zürich*, Heft, 9, pp. 1–195. Zürich, 1931.

—— "Pollenanalytische Untersuchungen an Mooren des Wallis," *Vierteljahrsschrift der Naturforschenden Gesellschaft in Zürich*, 1/2, pp. 18–71, Zürich, 1935.

KINZL, H. "Die grössten nacheiszeitlichen Gletschervorstösse in den Schweizer Alpen und in der Mont Blanc-Gruppe," *Zeitschrift für Gletscherkunde, für Eiszeitforschung und Geschichte des Klimas*, Band XX, pp. 269–397. Leipzig, 1932.

MANTEYER, GEORGES DE. "La traversée des Alpes par Hannibal," *Bulletin de la Société d'Etudes des Hautes Alpes*, 64, 1945, pp. 1–27.

—— "La voie fluviale du Rhone," *ibid.*, pp. 398–437.

MONTANARI, T. *Annibale*, Rovigo, 1890.

MONTERIN, UMBERTO. "Il clima sulle Alpi ha mutato in epoca storica?" *Consiglio nazionale delle ricerche. Comitato nazionale per la geografia*. II. *Ricerche sulle variazioni storiche del clima italiano*, 2. Bologna, 1937.

PARDÉ, MAURICE. *Le régime du Rhône. Etude hydrologique*. Lyon, 1925.

POST, VON L. "The prospect of pollen analysis in the study of the earth's climatic history," *The New Phytologist*, 45, 2, pp. 193–217. Cambridge, 1944.

SCULLARD, H. H. "Hannibal's Elephants," *Numismatic Chronicle*, 6th Series, 8, 1948, pp. 158–68.

STRACHAN-DAVIDSON, J. L. *Selections from Polybius*, pp. 15–21. Oxford, 1888.

TORR, C. *Hannibal Crosses the Alps*. Cambridge, 1935.

WISEMAN, J. D. H. "The determination and significance of past temperature changes in the upper layer of the Equatorial Atlantic Ocean," *Proceedings of the Royal Society of London*, Series A, 222, 1954, pp. 296–323.

REFERENCES

(References to classical authors quoted in the text. I have limited them to 100.)

1. Cornelius Nepos, *Hannibal*, 13.3. Sosilos taught Hannibal Greek.
2. Cicero, *De Divinatione*, i. 24. Silenos translated by Coelius.
3. Livy, xxi. 38.7. Coelius quoted.
4. Livy, xxi. 38.3. Hannibal's army's casualties.
5. Polybius, iii. 48.12. Polybius followed Hannibal's route.
6. Ammianus Marcellinus, xv. 10.11. Quotes Timagenes on Hannibal's route.
7. Silius Italicus, *Punica*, iii. 442–76. Hannibal's route.
8. Servius, *Ad Aeneidem*, x. 13. Quotes Varro on the passes of the Alps.
9. Polybius, iii, 49.5. Description of "the Island".
10. Livy, xxi. 31.4. Description of "the Island".
11. Polybius, iii. 49.6. The *Skaras*.
12. Livy, xxi. 31.4. The *Arar*.
13. Livy, xxi. 31.4. The *Arar* rises in the Alps.
14. Livy, xxi. 31.4. The name of "the Island".
15. Polybius, iii. 50.1. Hannibal's speed averages 80 stadia a day.
16. Polybius, iii. 39. 6–10. Distances covered by Hannibal.
17. Polybius, iii. 39.8. Interpolation making 8 stadia equal to one Roman mile.
18. Strabo, vii. 7.4. States that Polybius counted $8\frac{1}{3}$ stadia to the Roman mile.
19. Polybius, iii. 42.1. Hannibal crosses the Rhone where it is a single stream.
20. Strabo, iv. 1.3. The crossing of the Rhone at Tarascon.
21. Polybius, iii. 42–6. Description of the crossing of the Rhone.
22. Polybius, iii. 46.1. How the elephants were got across.
23. Livy, v. 34. Bellovesus' and other Gauls' crossing of the Alps.

113

24. Polybius, ii. 22.2. Concolitanus's and Aneroestus's crossing of the Alps.

25. Polybius, iii. 47.1. Hannibal marches up the east bank of the Rhone.

26. Strabo, iv. 1.7. Description of the plain of La Crau.

27. Aeschylus, frag. 199. *Prometheus unbound*, the pebbles of the plain of La Crau. Quoted by Strabo iv. 1.7.

28. Polybius, iii. 49.8–10; Livy, xxi. 31.6. Hannibal in "the Island".

29. Livy, xxi. 31.9. States that the inhabitants of "the Island" were Allobroges.

30. Livy, xxi. 31.5. States that the Allobroges lived near "the Island".

31. Polybius, iii. 49.13. Hannibal is given an escort to protect him from the Allobroges.

32. Polybius, iii. 50.1. The ascent on the way to the Alps.

33. Polybius, iii. 39.9. The ascent to the Alps.

34. Polybius, iii. 50.1. Hannibal's march from "the Island".

35. Livy, xxi. 31.9. Hannibal's march from "the Island".

36. Ammianus Marcellinus, xv. 10.11. quotes Timagenes's description of Hannibal's march.

37. Strabo, iv. 1.11. Location of the Gaulish tribes.

38. Ptolemy, *Geogr.*, ii, 10.12–19. Location of the Gaulish tribes.

39. Polybius, iii. 39.9. Hannibal's march beside the river.

40. Livy, xxi. 38.7. Quotes Coelius on the *Cremonis jugum*.

41. Cicero, *De Oratore* ii. 12.54. Praises Coelius.

42. Cicero, *De Divinatione* i. 24. States that Coelius obtained information from Silenos.

43. Livy, xxi. 38.6. Hannibal descends into the territory of the Taurini.

44. Livy, xxi. 31.9. Hannibal in the territories of the Tricastini, Vocontii, and Tricorii.

45. Polybius, iii. 51. Description of the first battle.

46. Livy, xxi. 31.9; and xxi. 33.1–10. Hannibal crosses the Durance and fights the first battle.

47. Livy, xxi. 31.12. The Durance in spate.

48. Strabo, iv. 6.12. The passes across the western Alps.

49. Servius, *Ad Aeneidem* x. 13. The passes across the western Alps.

50. Sallus, *Historiae*, frag. ii. 98. Pompey crossed a pass different from Hannibal's.
51. Appian, *De Bellis Civilibus* i. 13.109. Pompey's pass near the sources of the Rhone and the Po.
52. Strabo, iv. 6.5. The sources of tributaries of the Rhone and the Po.
53. Livy, xxvii. 39.7. Hasdrubal crossed Hannibal's pass.
54. Appian, *Hannibalica* vii. 52. Hasdrubal crossed Hannibal's pass.
55. Livy, xxi. 38.5–6. Everyone was agreed that Hannibal descended into the Territory of the Taurini.
56. Pliny, *Historia naturalis* iii. 17.123. Hercules crossed the Graian Alps.
57. Ptolemy, *Geogr.* iii. 1.39.40. Embrun and Briançon in the Graian Alps.
58. Cornelius Nepos, *Hannibal* 3.4. Hannibal crossed the Graian Alps.
59. Tacitus, *Historiae* ii. 66. The march over the Graian Alps from Turin.
60. Polybius, iii. 48.12. Polybius himself went by Hannibal's route over the Alps
61. Polybius, iii. 50–6. Narrative of Hannibal's march through the Alps.
62. Polybius, iii. 50.5. Hannibal encamps near the pass at the ascent towards the Alps.
63. Polybius, iii. 51.11. Hannibal captures the Gauls' town.
64. Livy, xxi. 33.11. Hannibal captures the Gauls' town.
65. Livy, xxi. 32.6. From the Gauls' town Hannibal marches through open country.
66. Polybius, iii. 53.5. The bivouac on the large bare rock.
67. Polybius, iii. 53.6. Hannibal approaches the highest pass of the Alps.
68. Livy, xxi. 35.4. Hannibal loses his way.
69. Polybius, iii. 54.1; and Livy, xxi. 35.6. The setting of the Pleiades.
70. Polybius, iii. 54.2; and Livy, xxi. 35.8. The view of Italy.
71. Polybius, i. 67.8. Carthaginian troops of many tongues.
72. Polybius, iii. 55.1. The snow on the pass.
73. Livy, xxi. 37.2. Ammianus Marcellinus xv. 10. Appian, *Hannibalica* i. 4. A rock split by fire and acid.

74. Polybius, iii. 56.4. Hannibal's losses.
75. Polybius, iii. 53.5. The bare rock.
76. Virgil, *Aeneid* x. 708. Monte Viso covered with pines.
77. Caesar, *De Bello Gallico* i. 10.4–5. Caesar's march into Gaul.
78. Appian, *De Rebus Gallicis*, vi. 1.3. Caesar's battle with the Tricorii.
79. Polybius, iii. 56.3. Hannibal descends from the Alps.
80. Ptolemy, *Geogr.* iii. 1.33. The territory of the Isubres.
81. Polybius, iii. 60.8–9. Hannibal captures the city of the Taurini.
82. Pliny, *Historia naturalis* xxiii. 27.57. Fire and vinegar disintegrate the rocks.
83. Pliny, xxxiii. 21.71. Stones cracked by fire and vinegar.
84. Vitruvius, viii. 3.19. Vinegar used to split stones.
85. Dion Cassius, xxxvi. 18.2. A tower destroyed by vinegar.
86. Polyaenus, *Strategematum* viii. 23.5. The elephant at the battle of London.
87. Florus, i. 22. Hannibal's campaign in Italy.
88. Polybius, iii. 74.11; iii. 79.12. All Hannibal's elephants die except one. Hannibal rides the last elephant.
89. Polybius, iii. 87.2; iii. 88.1. Hannibal cures his horses.
90. Hanno, *The Voyage of Hanno*, translated by T. Falconer. London, 1797; and Herodotus iv. 191. Elephants in Morocco.
91. Appian, *Punica*, ii. 9. Elephants in Morocco.
92. Suetonius Paulinus. Elephants in Morocco. Quoted by Pliny, *Historia Naturalis* v. 1.14.
93. Pliny, *Historia Naturalis* viii. 11. Elephants in Tunisia.
94. Polybius, iii. 46.7. Elephant drivers called Indians.
95. Pliny, viii. 5.11. The bravest elephant Surus.
96. Suetonius Tranquillus, *Nero* ii. 1. Elephants in Provence.
97. Lucius Junius Moderatus Columella, xi. 2.78. The setting of the Pleiades and the onset of winter.
98. Ptolemy, *Astron.* viii. 4. "Aspects" of stars.
99. Pliny, ii. 47.125. The setting of the Pleiades and the onset of winter.
100. Strabo, iv. 6.12. Quotes Polybius on the gold-mines of the High Tauern.

INDEX

MAP OF THE ALPS WHICH
HANNIBAL CROSSED

Hannibal's route was by Aigues Mortes to the Rhone which he crossed at Arles; by Maillane and across the Durance and the Aygues to "The Island"; "beside the river" by Donzère and Loriol to the Col de Grimone, the site of the First Battle; to the town in the neighbourhood of La Bâtie Montsaléon, and by Gap to the entrance to the valley of the Guil, site of the Second Battle; "the bare rock" at Château Queyras; to the Col de la Traversette and down to the plain of the Po at Saluzzo.

The Territory of the Tricastini is indicated by the letters *TR*.